Diet recommendations for diabetes mellitus

Please check these recommendations always with a nutrition consultant, therapist, doctor or dietician. The recipes and the list of ingredients are supporting the conventional medical therapy.
The calorie disclosures of fresh ingredients (fruit and vegetables) vary according to quality and time of harvest. The contents were checked by a dietician and a nutrition consultant for the Traditional Chinese Medicine (TCM).

Author:
©2019 Josef Miligui
www.ebns.at

AF236092

Source:
The lists are created from the EBNS database for nutritional counseling. The database is used by dietitians, therapists and doctors for advising the patient / client.

Literature:
The specialist literature and the training documents of the German and Austrian dietary and traditional Chinese medicine serve as a knowledge base. We have used the documents as a basis of knowledge, adapted it to our experience and completed them.
http://di-book.com

Production and publishing:
BoD – Books on Demand, Norderstedt
ISBN: 9783752861525

Diet recommendations for DIETETICS - Metabolism - Diabetes mellitus

1   Treatment strategy

Type I Diabetics need to inject the missing insulin and calculate and consume appropriate bread exchange unit (1 BEU) according to the prescribed insulin quantity.
For food therapy, BEU exchange tables are available, which

considerably facilitate the treatment of the disease.

The aim in the dietary therapy of a type II diabetic is to keep the insulin distributions as low as possible in order to improve stored energy, avoid hunger emotions and thus promote weight loss.

The basis is a healthy, balanced mixed food, whereby easily absorbable carbohydrates should be dispensed with if possible.

Whole grain products, abundant vegetables and moderate consumption of fruit and obsolete products are the main focus.

For both diabetes types moderate use of sugars is recommended (<10% of the daily energy - not in pure - isolated form).

Caution: Honey is 80% sugar.

Sugar substitutes (fructose, sugar alcohols) increase the blood glucose more slowly, but they have the same effect as pure sugar - they must therefore be avoided.

Artificial sweeteners do not have kcal, but should not be consumed excessively.

Stevia plant (sweet grass) as a sweetener can be used at your own risk after consultation with the doctor or therapist.

2   Avoid

Sugar and other easily absorbable carbohydrates such as White bread, noodles and rice.

Type II diabetic: calorie-rich and fatty foods and drinks, since they make the necessary weight reduction more difficult.

3   Breakfast

4 Snack

5 Lunch

6 Afternoon

7 Dinner

8   Any time

9 Recipes

(rec.) = You can use more.
(little) = You should use less than specified
(no) omit.

9.1 Andalusian fish pot

Strengthens immune system, prevents cancer, dissolves stagnation, promotes weight loss. Good to fight immunodeficiency, loss of appetite, flatulence, high blood pressure, depressions, diabetes, diarrhea, stimulates appetite.
Cooking time approx. 30 min
Allergens: ADLO
4 portions to 355g. / 348kcal. - (carb:71% / prot:29%)
100g.=97,96kcal. / protein 20,03g. fat:6,51g.
µg. - Ph:3,89 Na:5,05 Ka:8,67 Mg:3,36 Ca:10,73 Fe:0,03 Zn:0,02 Col.:0,79 Hsr.:2,47

Quantity of ingredients:
Basic recipe for a vegetable soup (nutritious) 2 cups / 500g. (yes)
Onion (spring onion) 2 pieces / 40g. (yes)
Olive oil 1 table spoon / 20g. (yes)
Lemon peel 1/2 piece / 3g. (yes)
Bay leaf 1 piece / 1g. (yes)
Potato 5/8 oz / 200g. (yes)
Cod 3/4 lbs / 300g. (yes)
White wine 4 table spoons / 80g. (little)
Lemon juice 1/2 teaspoon / 10g. (yes)
Salt 1 pinch / 1g. (little)
Pepper (ground) 1 pinch / 0,2g. ()
Parsley 1 table spoon / 15g. (yes)
White bread (wheat bread) 8 slices / 250g. (little)

Cooking instructions:
Boil the vegetable broth with small spring onion, olive oil, grated lemon peel and bay leaf. Boil covered for 10 minutes. Add the peeled, diced potatoes and boil in about 8 minutes. Add fish pieces and white wine and switch to
small heat. In the slightly boiling broth put the fish and boil it a few minutes. Season with lemon juice, salt and pepper. Serve with parsley sprinkled.
White bread as a side dish.

9.2 Antipasti

Improves blood circulation, anti-inflammatory, relieves pain. Diuretic, promotes digestion, reduces blood pressure, antioxidative, antibacterial, affects anorexia, improves digestion, flatulence, stomach weakness, stimulating.
Cooking time approx. 40 min
3 portions to 246,67g. / 100kcal. - (carb:54% / prot:46%)
100g.=40,54kcal. / protein 2,74g. fat:5,6g.
µg. - Ph:7,93 Na:1,08 Ka:67,54 Mg:5,14 Ca:7,21 Fe:0,24 Zn:0,03 Col.:0 Hsr.:5,8

Quantity of ingredients:
Pepperoni 1 piece / 5g. (yes)
Lemon juice 1 table spoon / 10g. (yes)
Aubergine 1 piece / 300g. (yes)
Tomato 4 pieces / 200g. (yes)
Zucchini 5/8 oz / 200g. (yes)
Lemon peel 1/2 piece / 3g. (yes)
Olive oil 1 table spoon / 15g. (yes)
Basil (fresh) 8 leaves / 5g. (yes)
Salt 1 pinch / 0,5g. (little)
Coriander 1/2 teaspoon / 2g. (yes)

Cooking instructions:
Preheat the oven to 250 degrees Celsius and bake the hot peppers until the bowl becomes dark (about 20 minutes). Cover the hot peppers with a clear film and allow to cool. Peel the skin and cut into strips about 2 cm wide. Cut tomatoes in half and spread with oil in slices of aubergine and bake in the oven at 200 degrees golden brown (about 10 minutes) Fry the zucchini slices in the grill pan (without fat).
Mix everything together, mix the marinade of olive oil, salt and lemon peel and pour over the vegetables, sprinkle with coriander. Leave for 1 hour.

9.3 Asparagus and herb ragout

Diuretic, improves blood circulation, prevents cancer, dissolves stagnation, promotes weight loss. Good to fight immunodeficiency, loss of appetite, flatulence, high blood pressure, depressions, diabetes, diarrhea, stimulates liver function.
Cooking time approx. 30 min
Allergens: GL

4 portions to 465,5g. / 168kcal. - (carb:78% / prot:22%)
100g.=36,14kcal. / protein 7,54g. fat:4,09g.
µg. - Ph:2,55 Na:0,54 Ka:11,94 Mg:2,69 Ca:9,45 Fe:0,06 Zn:0,02 Col.:0 Hsr.:1,09

Quantity of ingredients:
Basic recipe for a vegetable soup (nutritious) 2 cups / 500g. (yes)
Lemon peel 1/2 piece / 3g. (yes)
Coriander 1/4 teaspoon / 1g. (yes)
Nutmeg 1 pinch / 0,3g. (yes)
Asparagus (green or white) 1,8 lbs / 800g. (yes)
Parsley 1 Bunch / 125g. (yes)
Crème fraiche cheese 2 table spoons / 30g. (little)
Lemon juice 1 teaspoon / 3g. (yes)
Potato 7/8 lbs / 400g. (yes)

Cooking instructions:
Cook potatoes with plenty of salted water about 20 min. until soft.
Heat the vegetable stock with lemon zest, coriander and nutmeg till it
boil. Cook the peeled and sliced asparagus in it.
Drain asparagus in a sieve. Collect the cooking liquid.
In the blender mix 200 g of cooked asparagus (the lower ends), cooking
liquid and parsley to a smooth sauce. Beat the sauce with crème
fraîche until smooth. Add asparagus and heat again and season with
lemon juice, salt and pepper. Serve with the potatoes.

9.4   Basic recipe for a beef broth (clear)

Strengthens muscles, tendons and bones, reduces blood pressure,
strengthens immune system, prevents cancer, reduces radiation
damage, stimulates digestion, reduces pain, promotes digestion,
diuretic. Rosemary stimulates digestion.
Cooking time approx. 4-8 hours
Allergens: O
10 portions to 276g. / 114kcal. - (carb:22% / prot:78%)
100g.=41,41kcal. / protein 12,22g. fat:4,09g.
µg. - Ph:0,51 Na:0,31 Ka:1,34 Mg:0,11 Ca:0,25 Fe:0,01 Zn:0,01 Col.:0,14 Hsr.:0,36

Quantity of ingredients:
Beef soup meat 1,1 lbs / 500g. (little)
Beef meatbones 5/8 oz / 200g. (yes)
Vinegar (Red wine vinegar) 1 dash / 3g. (yes)
Juniper berry 8 pieces / 6g. (yes)

Rosemary 1 pinch / 1g. (yes)
Carrot 3 pieces / 210g. (yes)
Parsnip 2 pieces / 300g. (yes)
Leek 1 piece / 200g. (yes)
Ginger fresh 1/2 teaspoon / 5g. (yes)
Lovage 1 stem / 15g. (yes)
Clove 2 pieces / 2g. (yes)
Pimento 6 pieces / 12g. (yes)
Anise (Common Fennel) 2 pieces / 1g. (yes)
Salt 1 teaspoon / 5g. (little)
Water 3,3 lbs / 1300g. (yes)

Cooking instructions:
Heat water, a dash of red wine vinegar, some juniper berries, a little
rosemary, bones and meat till it boils; add carrot, parsnip, leek, ginger,
lovage, clove, allspice, star anise and a little salt; simmer for 4-8 hours
then strain.
Refrigerate for later use.

9.5   Basic recipe for a chicken broth worming

Strengthens blood, strengthens bone marrow, reduces blood pressure,
strengthens immune system, prevents cancer, reduces radiation
damage, promotes sweating, dissolves stagnation, good to fight loss of
appetite, flatulence.
Cooking time approx. 2-3 hours
Allergens: L
9 portions to 244,89g. / 90kcal. - (carb:10% / prot:90%)
100g.=36,66kcal. / protein 15,68g. fat:11,56g.
µg. - Ph:0,86 Na:0,59 Ka:1,87 Mg:0,13 Ca:0,38 Fe:0,01 Zn:0 Col.:0,25 Hsr.:0,92

Quantity of ingredients:
Chicken meat 1/2 piece / 600g. (yes)
Carrot 2 pieces / 150g. (yes)
Leek 1 stick / 45g. (yes)
Celery root 1 piece / 500g. (yes)
Ginger fresh 2 slices / 2g. (yes)
Fenugreek (Trigonella foenum-graecum) 1 teaspoon / 2g. (yes)
Juniper berry 1 teaspoon / 3g. (yes)
Bay leaf 3 pieces / 2g. (yes)
Water 4 cup / 900g. (yes)

Cooking instructions:
Remove chicken parts from fat. Place chicken pieces in a saucepan with hot water and heat till it boils briefly, skimming any resulting foam. Add coarsely chopped vegetables and all spices and cook over medium heat for 2 to 3 hours. Strain the finished soup. Throw away vegetables and bones.
Tip: If you want to use the meat as a soup insert, take out after 45 minutes and return only the bones in the soup.
Refrigerate for later use.

9.6   Basic recipe for a vegetable soup, nutritious

Reduces blood pressure, strengthens immune system, prevents cancer, forcing spleen, dissolves stagnation, promotes weight loss. Good to fight immunodeficiency, high blood pressure, depressions, diabetes, diarrhea, reduces blood lipids.
Cooking time approx. 2-3 hours
Allergens: L
5 portions to 240,6g. / 48kcal. - (carb:71% / prot:29%)
100g.=19,87kcal. / protein 1,56g. fat:1,31g.
µg. - Ph:0,97 Na:0,73 Ka:5,14 Mg:0,36 Ca:1,26 Fe:0,02 Zn:0,01 Col.:0 Hsr.:0,56

Quantity of ingredients:
Olive oil 1 table spoon / 4g. (yes)
Onion white 1 piece / 60g. (yes)
Carrot 3 pieces / 200g. (yes)
Parsnip 3/8 lbs - 6oz / 150g. (yes)
Celery root 1 cup / 100g. (yes)
Ginger fresh 1/2 teaspoon / 2g. (yes)
Lemon 1/2 piece / 25g. (yes)
Juniper berry 6 pieces / 6g. (yes)
Thyme dried 1 pinch / 1g. (yes)
Lovage 1 table spoon / 3g. (yes)
Bay leaf 2 leaves / 1g. (yes)
Salt 1 pinch / 1g. (little)
Water 3 cups / 650g. (yes)

Cooking instructions:
Cut the vegetables into cubes.
Heat oil in hot pot, fry shortly onions and vegetables.
Add cold water, then add ginger, bay leaf and lemon juice.
Season with juniper, thyme and lovage. Cover for 2 - 3 hours on a low heat and simmer.
The used vegetables should be thrown away.

The basic recipe serves as a soup base and to refine vegetables, legumes or cereals.
If you want to eat vegetable soup immediately, add the desired vegetables half an hour before.
Refrigerate for later use.

9.7 Bitter melon with tomato vegetables

Against diabetes in old age, constipation, infections. Promotes digestion, stimulates, warms, antispasmodic, appetizing.
Cooking time approx. 30 min.
Allergens: G
2 portions to 274,5g. / 176kcal. - (carb:47% / prot:53%)
100g.=64,3kcal. / protein 3,69g. fat:12,18g.
µg. - Ph:10,36 Na:3,24 Ka:55,42 Mg:5,01 Ca:10,32 Fe:0,17 Zn:0,05 Col.:0,26 Hsr.:1,9

Quantity of ingredients:
Bitter melon 2 pieces / 250g. (rec.)
Tomato 2 pieces / 200g. (yes)
Yogurt (natural, 3.5% fat) 4 table spoons / 40g. (little)
Corn germ oil 3 table spoons / 20g. (yes)
Lemon 1 piece / 5g. (yes)
Garlic 4 pieces / 5g. (yes)
Ginger fresh 1/2 oz / 10g. (yes)
Chili (pod or ground) 1/2 teaspoon / 2g. (yes)
Coriander 1 table spoon / 5g. (yes)
Cardamom 1 table spoon / 5g. (yes)
Cumin (Caraway seed) 1 table spoon / 5g. (yes)
Saffron 1g. Or 0,034oz / 1g. (yes)
Salt 1 pinch / 1g. (little)
Pepper (ground) 1 pinch / 0,5g. ()

Cooking instructions:
Cut the bitter melon in halfs, core it and cut it into strips. Then cut into small cubes. Cut the tomatoes into small pieces. Cut the chili into thin rings. Finely chop the garlic. Peel and finely slice the ginger.
In a saucepan with the oil, stir in the bitter cucumbers. Add tomatoes, garlic, ginger and salt. Simmer for 15 minutes. Stir in the spices and the lemon juice.

This fits rice or potatoes.

9.8   Breakfast - low protein

Increase appetite, detoxifying, increases blood glucose levels, harmonizes heart rhythm, good to fight vomiting, nutritional disorders, diarrhea.

Cooking time approx. 10 min

Allergens: GO

1 portion to 330g. / 575kcal. - (carb:69% / prot:31%)
100g.=174,24kcal. / protein 4,87g. fat:27,83g.
µg. - Ph:104,21 Na:225,52 Ka:58,03 Mg:6,12 Ca:26,88 Fe:0,27 Zn:0,23 Col.:15,74
Hsr.:47,27

Quantity of ingredients:
Bread with carob kernel flour 3 oz / 80g. (yes)
Butter organic 1/2 oz / 20g. (little)
Apricot jam 1 oz / 30g. (little)
Fresh cheese with herbs 1 oz / 30g. (yes)
Coffee 1/2 cup / 150g. (yes)
Sugar white 1/2 oz / 10g. (little)

Cooking instructions:
Prepare coffee to taste, make fresh cheese if possible with fresh herbs yourself.

9.9   Breakfast with cheese

Good to fight weakness, stomach pressure, belching, diabetes, acute or chronic obstruction of the bowel, skin problems. Coffee supports urinating, stimulates appetite, detoxifying, increases blood glucose levels, harmonizes heart rhythm.

Cooking time approx. 10 min

Allergens: AGO

1 portion to 364g. / 593kcal. - (carb:46% / prot:54%)
100g.=162,91kcal. / protein 22,49g. fat:34,96g.
µg. - Ph:139,8 Na:214,1 Ka:121 Mg:21,93 Ca:99,75 Fe:0,82 Zn:1,12 Col.:10,93
Hsr.:18,97

Quantity of ingredients:
Water 1 cup / 120g. (yes)
Coffee 2 teaspoons / 4g. (yes)
Whole grain bread 2 slices / 100g. (yes)
Margarine 1/2 oz / 10g. (yes)
Edam cheese 1 oz / 30g. (yes)
Strawberry jam 1/2 oz / 20g. (little)
Curd cheese 20% 1/8 lbs - 2oz / 40g. (yes)

Cooking instructions:
Prepare coffee as usual. Avoid sugar or use sweetener. Cover the bread slices with margarine and put the cheese and marmalade on the breakfast table. Decorating decoratively increases your appetite.

9.10 Bulgur with tomatoes and fresh herbs

Promotes digestion, helps to digest fat, supports urination, reduces blood pressure. Stimulates digestion, supports urination.
Cooking time approx. 30 min
Allergens: A
1 portion to 244g. / 205kcal. - (carb:71% / prot:29%)
100g.=84,02kcal. / protein 14,92g. fat:22,17g.
µg. - Ph:136,51 Na:6,27 Ka:256,14 Mg:48,22 Ca:20,11 Fe:1,82 Zn:1,3 Col.:0,08
Hsr.:78,86

Quantity of ingredients:
Bulgur (cereals) 1 cup / 120g. (yes)
Tomato 2 pieces / 70g. (yes)
Rucola 2 table spoons / 16g. ()
Pepper powder (hot) 1 pinch / 2g. (yes)
Olive oil 2 table spoons / 20g. (yes)
Pepper (ground) 1 pinch / 0,5g. ()
Salt 1 pinch / 1g. (little)
Basil 4 leaves / 2g. (yes)
Thyme 1 Twig / 3g. (yes)
Lemon juice 1/2 piece / 10g. (yes)

Cooking instructions:
Put cold water in a pot, sprinkle in Bulgur and simmer. Stir in chopped tomatoes, fresh herbs like basil, thyme, arugula, a pinch of rose paprika, lemon juice, a dash of olive oil, a little ground pepper, some salt.

Variant: add some mozzarella.

Recommendation: ideal morning meal in summer; also suitable as evening meal, especially for sleep disorders.

9.11 Casserole with white cabbage and apples

Stimulates blood production and metabolism, promotes digestion, appetite stimulating, strengthens the stomach, triggers stagnation, slightly laxative, reduces fat.
Cooking time approx. 2 hours and more
Allergens: CGL

3 portions to 446g. / 252kcal. - (carb:59% / prot:41%)
100g.=56,5kcal. / protein 10,67g. fat:12,62g.
µg. - Ph:17,65 Na:9,84 Ka:49,36 Mg:10,37 Ca:38,36 Fe:0,2 Zn:0,11 Col.:12,63 Hsr.:3,96

Quantity of ingredients:
White cabbage / 500g. (yes)
Onion white / 50g. (yes)
Rapeseed oil / 10g. (yes)
Water / 25g. (yes)
Basic recipe for a vegetable soup (nutritious) / 200g. (yes)
Salt / 1g. (little)
Pepper (ground) / 0,5g. ()
Ground caraway / 2g. (yes)
Apple (sweet) / 200g. (little)
Chicken egg / 120g. (yes)
Cow's milk (1.5% fat) / 180g. (yes)
Sour cream 15% fat / 50g. (little)

Cooking instructions:
Preheat the oven to 180 ° C (circulating air: 160 ° C). Clean white cabbage, quarter and remove the stalk. Cut the herb into fine strips. Peel onions, halve and cut into thin rings. Heat oil in a tall pot and fry onion rings first and then roast the herb. Mix water with vegetable soup and pour on. Cook with the lid closed for about 15 minutes on a medium flame. Season with salt, pepper and cumin.
Wash apple, quarter, core. Cut into slices and place under the herb. Whisk eggs with milk, salt and pepper. Put the mixture in a casserole dish and pour the egg milk over it. Bake in preheated tube, golden brown for 40 to 50 minutes. Smooth the sour cream. Portion the casserole on a plate and add a small amount of sour cream each time.

9.12 Celery and potato cream soup

Reduces blood pressure, strengthens immune system, promotes weight loss. Good to fight immunodeficiency, loss of appetite, flatulence, depressions, diabetes, diarrhea, improves digestion.
Cooking time approx. 45 min
Allergens: GL
4 portions to 241,5g. / 113kcal. - (carb:83% / prot:17%)
100g.=46,69kcal. / protein 2,15g. fat:5,52g.
µg. - Ph:5,96 Na:3,46 Ka:23,98 Mg:22,27 Ca:83,51 Fe:0,18 Zn:0,01 Col.:0 Hsr.:1,49

Quantity of ingredients:
Olive oil 1 table spoon / 10g. (yes)
Onion white 1/2 piece / 25g. (yes)
Basic recipe for a vegetable soup (nutritious) 3 cups / 700g. (yes)
Potato 5/8 oz / 200g. (yes)
Nutmeg 1 pinch / 0,5g. (yes)
Ground 1 pinch / 0,5g. (yes)
Lemon peel 1/4 piece / 1g. (yes)
Crème fraiche cheese 2 table spoons / 20g. (little)
Salt 1 pinch / 1g. (little)
Parsley 1 table spoon / 8g. (yes)

Cooking instructions:
Heat the olive oil in a saucepan lightly. Fry the onions very gently in a mild heat. Pour with vegetable stock according to the basic recipe. Cover and cook for 15 minutes.
Add curd-cut potato, celery, nutmeg, cumin and lemon zest. Spice with salt and cook for 12 minutes. Potatoes and celery should be soft. Remove the lemon peel.
Puree the soup with crème fraiche using a blender. Season the soup with salt. Arrange the soup in portions with the chopped parsley.

9.13 Chicken soup with green spelt, parsley and sake

Strengthens blood, strengthens bone marrow, reduces blood pressure, strengthens immune system, stimulates liver function, detoxifying. Improves blood circulation, improves medication effect, stimulates appetite.
Cooking time approx. 1 1/2 hours
Allergens: AL
2 portions to 273g. / 150kcal. - (carb:84% / prot:16%)
100g.=54,95kcal. / protein 17,19g. fat:1,3g.
µg. - Ph:9,83 Na:8,28 Ka:15,94 Mg:25,41 Ca:66,21 Fe:0,3 Zn:0,08 Col.:0,45 Hsr.:3,87

Quantity of ingredients:
Basic recipe for a chicken soup (warming) 2 cup / 500g. (yes)
Green spelt 4 table spoons / 30g. (yes)
Parsley 2 table spoons / 14g. (yes)
Sake 1 dash / 2g. (yes)

Cooking instructions:
Cook the chicken broth according to the basic recipe. Add the ingredients in the soup and simmer 10 min.

9.14 Cocoa with cardamom

Builds up liver, strengthens muscles, lowers blood pressure. Antioxidant, rich in vital substances. Slightly laxative. Promotes digestion.
Cooking time approx. 5 min.
Allergens: G
2 portions to 533g. / 350kcal. - (carb:66% / prot:34%)
100g.=65,67kcal. / protein 17,84g. fat:8,81g.
µg. - Ph:60,04 Na:23,87 Ka:116,01 Mg:15,45 Ca:59,34 Fe:0,35 Zn:0,16 Col.:1,41
Hsr.:0,49

Quantity of ingredients:
Cocoa 50 g. / 50g. (yes)
Vanilla pod 1 piece / 0,5g. (yes)
Cow's milk (1.5% fat) 4 cup / 1000g. (yes)
Sugar white 4 table spoons / 15g. (little)
Cardamom 1 pinch / 1g. (yes)

Cooking instructions:
Mix the cocoa powder with the sugar, the pith of the vanilla pod, cardamom and 4-5 tablespoons of cold milk. Heat the milk in a pan (do not boil), stir in the cocoa with the whisk.

9.15 Colorful rice dish

Strengthens immune system, good to fight diabetes, strengthens spleen and stomach, strengthens blood, strengthens the muscles, tendons and bones, promotes digestion, helps to digest fat, supports urination, reduces blood pressure, dissolves stagnation.

Cooking time approx. 45 min

Allergens: L

3 portions to 342,67g. / 437kcal. - (carb:63% / prot:37%)
100g.=127,63kcal. / protein 17,03g. fat:10,23g.
µg. - Ph:7,97 Na:4,89 Ka:17,25 Mg:6,38 Ca:18,08 Fe:0,14 Zn:0,11 Col.:1 Hsr.:5,14

Quantity of ingredients:
Olive oil 2 teaspoons / 20g. (yes)
Onion (spring onion) 1 piece / 20g. (yes)
Beef meat 1/4 lbs - 4oz / 125g. (yes)
Rice (whole grain) 3 oz / 80g. (yes)
Basic recipe for a vegetable soup (nutritious) 1 cup / 300g. (yes)
Celery root 1/8 lbs - 2oz / 50g. (yes)
Leek 1 piece / 100g. (yes)
Beans (green, fresh) 3/8 lbs - 6oz / 150g. (yes)
Carrot 1 piece / 70g. (yes)
Tomato 2 pieces / 100g. (yes)
Salt 1 pinch / 0,5g. (little)
Pepper (ground) 1 pinch / 0,2g. ()
Herbs various 2 table spoons / 12g. (yes)

Cooking instructions:
Wash leek and carrots, clean and chop them. Dice the celery, slice the tomatoes.

Fry in a large, deep pan with oil, onion and minced meat.

Add brown rice and prepared vegetables (celery, leeks, beans, carrots, tomatoes). Braise briefly.

Season with salt, pepper and paprika. Add vegetable broth. Heat till it boils and cook over low heat for 20 to 30 minutes with the lid closed.

Sprinkle with fresh chopped herbs and serve.

9.16 Cream cheese substitute

Good to fight lactose intolerance. Strengthens body energy, promotes digestion, promotes weight loss. Good to fight immunodeficiency, loss of appetite, arteriosclerosis, flatulence, bladder weakness, anemia, high blood pressure, depressions, diabetes, diarrhea.
Cooking time approx. 20 min
Allergens: AE
2 portions to 328g. / 526kcal. - (carb:64% / prot:36%)
100g.=160,37kcal. / protein 19,62g. fat:12,75g.
µg. - Ph:32,54 Na:139,79 Ka:55,62 Mg:9,78 Ca:5,31 Fe:0,41 Zn:0,33 Col.:0 Hsr.:16,16

Quantity of ingredients:
Soybean milk 4 cup / 300g. (yes)
Lemon 1 piece / 50g. (yes)
Herbs various 2 table spoons / 6g. (yes)
Whole grain bread 6 slices / 300g. (yes)

Cooking instructions:
Heat the soy milk in a saucepan till it boils, stirring occasionally (gets burn easily!), Then allow to cool.
Squeeze out the lemon and stir gently under the cooled soy milk (approx. 80°C/176°F), let it approx. 20 min. rest or clot.
Pour chopped soy milk through a strainer lined with a dishcloth, allow liquid to drain and then squeeze out remaining liquid with the dishcloth.
Refine to taste with fresh herbs.
Serve with bread from carob kernel flour.

9.17 Cucumber salad

Diuretic, detoxifying, suppresses conversion of sugar into fat, lowers cholesterol, prevents cancer. Cucumber cools and moistens. Dill works against flatulence, anticonvulsant in gastrointestinal discomfort.
Cooking time approx. 5 min
Allergens: O
2 portions to 206g. / 27kcal. - (carb:68% / prot:32%)
100g.=13,11kcal. / protein 1,61g. fat:0,4g.
µg. - Ph:5,92 Na:2,32 Ka:35,15 Mg:2,16 Ca:4,03 Fe:0,12 Zn:0,05 Col.:0 Hsr.:1,94

Quantity of ingredients:
Cucumber 1 piece / 400g. (yes)
Salt 1 pinch / 1g. (little)
Dill 1 pinch / 1g. (yes)
Vinegar (Apple vinegar) 1 table spoon / 10g. (yes)

Cooking instructions:
Cut the cucumber (do not peel the BIO) thinly and season.

9.18 Cucumber soup

Diuretic, detoxifying, suppresses conversion of sugar into fat, lowers cholesterol, prevents cancer, promotes digestion, diaphoretic, dries out, good to fight yeast infections.
Cooking time approx. 20 min
Allergens: M
4 portions to 235,25g. / 96kcal. - (carb:22% / prot:78%)
100g.=40,6kcal. / protein 0,91g. fat:9,03g.
µg. - Ph:2,67 Na:1,28 Ka:15,6 Mg:1,17 Ca:2,57 Fe:0,06 Zn:0,01 Col.:0 Hsr.:0,85

Quantity of ingredients:
Olive oil 2 table spoons / 35g. (yes)
Cucumber 2 pieces / 400g. (yes)
Water 2 cup / 500g. (yes)
Sage 3 leaves / 3g. (yes)
Mustard 1/2 teaspoon / 0,5g. (yes)
Coriander 1 pinch / 1g. (yes)
Cardamom 1 pinch / 1g. (yes)
Salt 1 pinch / 1g. (little)

Cooking instructions:
Heat oil and roast short the small cucumbers. Add Mustard seeds, coriander, cardamom and salt. Add water. Simmer for 10-15 min. Puree and decorate with fresh chopped sage.

9.19 Exotic lenses

Strengthens heart and kidney, diuretic, calms the stomach, promotes digestion, dissolves stagnation, helps to digest fat, supports urination, reduces blood pressure, detoxifying and stimulating the immune system.
Cooking time approx. 45 min
Allergens: NO
4 portions to 273,25g. / 144kcal. - (carb:71% / prot:29%)
100g.=52,61kcal. / protein 5,82g. fat:3,45g.
µg. - Ph:13,57 Na:11,6 Ka:48,37 Mg:8,53 Ca:8,91 Fe:0,27 Zn:0,02 Col.:0 Hsr.:13,4

Quantity of ingredients:
Sesame oil 1 table spoon / 10g. (yes)
Onion white 2 pieces / 120g. (yes)
Ginger fresh 1/2 teaspoon / 2g. (yes)
Thyme dried 1/2 teaspoon / 1g. (yes)
Cumin (Caraway seed) 1/2 teaspoon / 2g. (yes)
Lentils red 1 cup / 120g. (yes)
Wakame 1 inch / 1g. (yes)
Lemon 1/2 piece / 20g. (yes)
Bocksdorn fruits (Fructus Lycii, goji berry dried 2 pinches / 2g. (yes)
Sugar cane sugar 1 pinch / 1g. (little)
Chili (pod or ground) 1 pinch / 0,5g. (yes)
Salt 1 pinch / 1g. (little)
Vinegar (Apple vinegar) 1/2 teaspoon / 1g. (yes)
Tomato 1 piece / 50g. (yes)
Chard 5/8 oz / 200g. (little)
Cauliflower 5/8 oz / 200g. (yes)
Salt 1 pinch / 1g. (little)
Rice (whole grain) 1/2 cup / 60g. (yes)
Water 3 cups / 300g. (yes)
Salt 1 pinch / 1g. (little)

Cooking instructions:
Heat sesame oil in a hot pot. Add chopped onions, grated ginger, dried thyme, plenty of cumin and sauté gently. Add peeled red lentils, a strip of wakame, a little lemon juice, hot water and some dried buckthorn fruits. Simmer for 20 minutes until the lentils are cooked; add hot water as needed to make a pulp. Add sugar, some chili and salt. Add vinegar or lemon juice depending on your taste. Add chopped tomatoes as desired. Let it pass for a few minutes.

Cook in a small pot with 1 cup of water and a little salt the cauliflower 10 min. until soft.
Blanch in a small pot with 1 cup of water and salt the chard 3 min.

Boil the rice briefly, salt and 10 min. to let go. Serve everything with the lentil dish.

9.20 Fennel and potato gratin

Reduces inflammation, improves blood circulation, improves digestion, supports urination, lowers cholesterol, good to fight loss of appetite, flatulence, inflammatory bowel disease, heartburn. Forcing spleen, improves blood circulation.

Cooking time approx. 1 1/2 hours

Allergens: CGL

2 portions to 230,5g. / 147kcal. - (carb:68% / prot:32%)
100g.=63,77kcal. / protein 5,72g. fat:5,42g.
µg. - Ph:15 Na:12,98 Ka:80,91 Mg:13,52 Ca:40,41 Fe:0,41 Zn:0,09 Col.:7,81 Hsr.:3,64

Quantity of ingredients:
Fennel 5/8 oz / 200g. (yes)
Potato 1/4 lbs - 4oz / 125g. (yes)
Basic recipe for a vegetable soup (nutritious) 1/2 cup / 100g. (yes)
Butter organic 1 teaspoon / 3g. (little)
Rice flour 2 teaspoons / 6g. (yes)
Cream sour 10% 1 teaspoon / 3g. (yes)
Salt 1 pinch / 1g. (little)
Sugar cane sugar 1 pinch / 1g. (little)
Chicken yolk 1 piece / 10g. (yes)
Pepper Cayenne 1 pinch / 0,5g. (yes)
Nutmeg 1 pinch / 0,5g. (yes)
Parsley 1 teaspoon / 2g. (yes)
Chives 1 teaspoon / 3g. (yes)
Parmesan 1 teaspoon / 3g. (little)
Butter organic 1 teaspoon / 3g. (little)

Cooking instructions:
Cook peeled potatoes and then let cool. Wash the fennel, cut off the stems and remove any outer leaves.
Hold back fennel greens and add it to the sauce with the other herbs later.
Steam the fennel tubers for about 15 - 20 minutes.
Then cut the potatoes and fennel into slices and place in layers in a greased baking dish.
Bring the liquid of fennel broth to the boil and bind it with flour.
Season with sea salt, cayenne pepper, sugar, nutmeg and sour cream. Allow to cool and alloy with egg yolk.
Spread the sauce over the casserole, sprinkle with parmesan and finely chopped parsley and chives. Bake at 200 °C / 392 °F in the oven for half an hour.

9.21 Fennel with roasted walnuts

Forcing spleen, detoxifying, reduces inflammation, improves blood circulation, improves medication effect, stimulates
appetite, antioxidative, promotes digestion, stimulates, dissolves stagnation.
Cooking time approx. 20 min
Allergens: HO
4 portions to 336,25g. / 342kcal. - (carb:54% / prot:46%)
100g.=101,78kcal. / protein 8,83g. fat:16,41g.
µg. - Ph:3,06 Na:3,38 Ka:20,35 Mg:2,24 Ca:4,39 Fe:0,11 Zn:0,02 Col.:0 Hsr.:0,88

Quantity of ingredients:
Fennel 4 pieces / 800g. (yes)
Nutmeg 1 pinch / 1g. (yes)
Ginger fresh 1/2 teaspoon / 1g. (yes)
Salt 1 pinch / 1g. (little)
White wine 1/2 cup / 125g. (little)
Peppers powder 1 pinch / 1g. (yes)
Olive oil 2 table spoons / 40g. (yes)
Walnuts 2 table spoons / 35g. (yes)
Water 1 1/2 cups / 220g. (yes)
Corn Grease (Polenta) 1 cup / 120g. (yes)
Salt 1 pinch / 1g. (little)

Cooking instructions:
Heat very little water in a pot; Fry the fennel in strips. Add Nutmeg, a little grated ginger, add salt, a dash of white wine, rose paprika.
Simmer until the vegetables are cooked, but still crisp; stir in a little olive oil; sprinkle with roasted walnuts.
Stir the polenta into a pot of hot water, stirring constantly, until the polenta has the desired consistency. Salt.
Pull the polenta off the fire and let it swell for about 10 minutes.

9.22 Figs with mozzarella and honey

Promotes digestion, reduces inflammation, bloating and nausea, relaxing and reassuring, relieves pain, detoxifying, blood stilling, forcing spleen and digestive system, detoxifying, bactericide.
Cooking time approx. 10 min
Allergens: GO
1 portion to 248g. / 415kcal. - (carb:52% / prot:48%)
100g.=167,34kcal. / protein 13,15g. fat:22,64g.
µg. - Ph:84,6 Na:105,09 Ka:195,74 Mg:16,03 Ca:153,4 Fe:0,55 Zn:0,52 Col.:9,27 Hsr.:6,05

Quantity of ingredients:
Fig 4 pieces / 100g. (yes)
Mozzarella 1 piece / 50g. (yes)
Basil (fresh) 1/2 bunch / 50g. (yes)
Honey 2 table spoons / 24g. (little)
Pepper (ground) 1 pinch / 0,1g. ()
Grapeseed oil 1 table spoon / 12g. (yes)
Vinegar Aceto Balsamico white 1 table spoon / 12g. (yes)

Cooking instructions:
Quarter fresh figs, dice buffalo mozzarella, pluck basil leaves.
Mix a dressing with light balsamic vinegar, grapeseed oil and honey and season to taste.
Place the figs on the edge of the appropriate plate. Spread the mozzarella cubes and season with black pepper. Spread whole or roughly sliced basil leaves over it and moisten with the marinade.
Bread with carob kernel flour goes perfectly with it.

9.23 Halibut with tomato and garlic sauce

Promotes digestion, helps to digest fat, supports urination, reduces blood pressure, good to fight rheumatism, flatulence, bladder weakness, anemia, high blood pressure, depressions, diabetes, diarrhea. Valuable omega-3 fatty acids.
Cooking time approx. 45 min
Allergens: D
5 portions to 297,6g. / 319kcal. - (carb:36% / prot:64%)
100g.=107,19kcal. / protein 34,96g. fat:9,44g.
µg. - Ph:4,82 Na:8,78 Ka:7,08 Mg:1,03 Ca:0,88 Fe:0,02 Zn:0,01 Col.:0,82 Hsr.:4,78

Quantity of ingredients:
Rice variety any 1 cup / 120g. (yes)
Water 6 cups / 240g. (yes)
Salt 1 pinch / 1g. (little)
Halibut (Flatfish) 2,2 lbs / 800g. (yes)
Salt 1 pinch / 1g. (little)
Pepper (ground) 1 pinch / 0,5g. ()
Lemon juice 1 splash / 2g. (yes)
Bay leaf 2 pieces / 2g. (yes)
Lemon 1 piece / 30g. (yes)
Garlic 8 pieces / 10g. (yes)

Thyme dried 1 table spoon / 5g. (yes)
Olives 0,2 lbs / 75g. (yes)
Tomato 4 pieces / 200g. (yes)
Salt 1 pinch / 1g. (little)
Pepper (ground) 1 pinch / 0,5g. ()

Cooking instructions:
Cook rice with salted water (1:3).
Rinse the fish under running cold water, dab with kitchen paper and rub with salt, pepper and lemon juice.
Place the fish fillets in a casserole dish with pieces of bay leaf.

Wash the lemon hot and cut into slices, peel and halve the garlic.
Sprinkle the olives and the thyme over them.
Brew the tomatoes with hot water, skin and chop.

Mix all ingredients, season with salt and pepper and distribute around the fish.
Cook everything at 200°C/392°F for about 20 minutes.
Serve with the rice.

9.24 Jerusalem artichokes with chive sauce

Strengthens the immune system, reduces fat, promotes appetite, improves digestion and blood circulation. Good for acute or chronic constipation.
Cooking time approx. 30 minutes
Allergens: ACG
2 portions to 426g. / 214kcal. - (carb:82% / prot:18%)
100g.=50,23kcal. / protein 15,17g. fat:7,98g.
µg. - Ph:46,12 Na:13,82 Ka:180,47 Mg:9,26 Ca:28,06 Fe:1,16 Zn:0,3 Col.:14,68 Hsr.:5,02

Quantity of ingredients:
Topinambur / 500g. ()
Chicken egg / 60g. (yes)
Wheat flour whole grain / 7g. (yes)
Salt / 1g. (little)
Pepper (ground) / 0,5g. ()
Nutmeg / 0,2g. (yes)
Rapeseed oil / 3g. (yes)
Yogurt (natural, 1.5% fat) / 250g. (yes)
Salt / 1g. (little)
Chives / 30g. (yes)

Cooking instructions:
The Jerusalem artichokes are washed well under running water. Then they are unpeeled grated with a fine grater.

The porridge is stirred in a bowl with the flour and egg and seasoned with salt, pepper and nutmeg.
A shot of rapeseed oil is then heated in a pan and, depending on the desired size, one or more spoons of the Jerusalem artichoke pulp are placed in the heated pan. The mixture is then pressed flat with the spoon and sautéed from both sides for 4 minutes until golden brown.
In a bowl, mix the yoghurt with chopped chives and salt.
Arrange the camisole and place the sauce next to it.

9.25 Kohlrabi in chervil sauce with potatoes

Reduces inflammation, lowers cholesterol, diuretic, conducts bowel winds, strengthens immune system, prevents cancer, promotes weight loss. Good to fight loss of appetite, flatulence, high blood pressure, depressions, diabetes, diarrhea.
Cooking time approx. 1 hour
Allergens: GL
4 portions to 316,75g. / 188kcal. - (carb:79% / prot:21%)
100g.=59,19kcal. / protein 8,66g. fat:2,51g.
µg. - Ph:2,95 Na:1,03 Ka:25,06 Mg:3,48 Ca:15,16 Fe:0,04 Zn:0,02 Col.:0,06 Hsr.:0,91

Quantity of ingredients:
Potato 6 pieces / 450g. (yes)
Basic recipe for a vegetable soup (nutritious) 1 cup / 300g. (yes)
Potato 1/4 lbs - 4oz / 100g. (yes)
Nutmeg 1 pinch / 0,2g. (yes)
Lemon peel 1/2 teaspoon / 2g. (yes)
Ginger fresh 1/2 teaspoon / 2g. (yes)
Lovage 1/2 teaspoon / 2g. (yes)
Kohlrabi 3/4 lbs / 300g. (yes)
Salt 1 pinch / 1g. (little)
Pepper (ground) 1 pinch / 0,2g. ()
Sour cream 15% fat 3 table spoons / 30g. (little)
Chervil dried 1 Bunch / 80g. (yes)

Cooking instructions:
Boil the potatoes in salted water.
Bring half of the vegetable stock to boil. Add the diced potatoes, nutmeg, lemon zest, ginger and lovage. Cover the potatoes and cook for about 10 minutes until soft and puree them with a blender until they are smooth.
Bring remaining vegetable stock to boil. Cut kohlrabi into cubes and add, cover and cook for about 8 minutes. Stir in the potato sauce and heat everything briefly.
Puree with the mixing stick chervil and sour cream. Mix the chervil cream with the kohlrabi vegetables.
Serve with the cooked, peeled potatoes.

9.26 Lentil and chestnut soup with curry

Reduces blood pressure, strengthens immune system, prevents cancer, reduces radiation damage, dissolves stagnation, promotes weight loss.
Good to loss of appetite, flatulence, diabetes, diarrhea.
Cooking time approx. 45 min
Allergens: LO
4 portions to 238,25g. / 175kcal. - (carb:83% / prot:17%)
100g.=73,45kcal. / protein 4,17g. fat:4,33g.
µg. - Ph:2,67 Na:3,8 Ka:7,98 Mg:4,63 Ca:15,86 Fe:0,06 Zn:0,02 Col.:0 Hsr.:2,07

Quantity of ingredients:
Lentils red 3/8 lbs - 6oz / 150g. (yes)
Chestnuts 3/8 lbs - 6oz / 150g. (yes)
Olive oil 1 table spoon / 10g. (yes)
Curry 2 teaspoons / 8g. (yes)
Turmeric (yellow root) 1 teaspoon / 2g. (yes)
Basic recipe for a vegetable soup (nutritious) 2 cup / 500g. (yes)
White wine 1/2 cup / 125g. (little)
Salt (herbal) 1 pinch / 1g. (little)
Anise (Common Fennel) 1 pinch / 1g. (yes)
Cardamom 1 pinch / 0,5g. (yes)
Parsley 2 table spoons / 6g. (yes)

Cooking instructions:
Add the olive oil to a pan, sauté the chestnuts, sprinkle with the curry, add the lentils and season with vegetable stock, add a little white wine, mix in the curcuma, simmer for about 20 minutes (until the chestnuts are tender).
Then puree the soup. Taste with a pinch of anise, cardamom and herbal salt. At the end, sprinkle finely chopped parsley over it.

9.27 Marinated turkey with cashew nuts from the wok

Strengthens blood, strengthens bone marrow, for the drainage of the body overweight and high blood pressure. Promotes digestion, helps to digest fat, supports urination, reduces blood pressure.
Cooking time approx. 30 min
Allergens: ELNO
4 portions to 329,25g. / 319kcal. - (carb:55% / prot:45%)
100g.=96,89kcal. / protein 21,49g. fat:10,29g.
µg. - Ph:22,19 Na:6,37 Ka:34,04 Mg:8,67 Ca:9,27 Fe:0,18 Zn:0,17 Col.:3,47 Hsr.:10,46

Quantity of ingredients:
Turkey breast meat 3/4 lbs / 300g. (yes)
Sake until covered / 5g. (yes)
Sesame oil 2 table spoons / 30g. (yes)
Ginger fresh 1/2 teaspoon / 2g. (yes)
Salt 1 pinch / 0,5g. (little)
Lemon 1/2 piece / 15g. (yes)
Red wine 1/2 cup / 125g. (yes)
Sugar cane sugar 1 pinch / 1g. (little)
Onion (spring onion) 4 pieces / 80g. (yes)
Tomato 2 pieces / 100g. (yes)
Basic recipe for a chicken soup (warming) 1 cup / 120g. (yes)
Cashews 2 table spoons / 16g. (yes)
Soy sauce 1 dash / 2g. (yes)
Rice Basmati 1 cup / 120g. (yes)
Water 6 cups / 400g. (yes)
Salt 1 pinch / 0,5g. (little)

Cooking instructions:
Preparation: cover sliced turkey meat with rice wine; marinate overnight or for a few hours.
Then: strain and drain well; heat sesame oil in a hot wok; fry finely chopped ginger; sauté the meat for a short time;
add the marinade; add salt, lemon juice, red wine or rose paprika; let the meat soak in the sauce for 2 - 3 minutes; then exhaust it; add some sugar to the sauce in the wok; add a few spring onions (the white parts), a pinch of salt, chopped tomatoes, 1 cup of chicken broth; simmer so that the onions are still crisp.
Roasted cashews, add the cashews and the meat to the sauce and heat; season with soy sauce; stir in the green
of the chopped green onions.
Boil the rice with the water, salt and cook for about 20 minutes.

9.28 Millet with pears

Refreshing and nourishing, promotes digestion, supports urination, good to fight cough, promotes perspiration, reduces blood lipids, stimulates, dissolves stagnation, forces liver, strengthens the muscles, lowers cholesterol, antiparasitic.
Cooking time approx. 35 min
Allergens: G
5 portions to 238,4g. / 213kcal. - (carb:86% / prot:14%)
100g.=89,43kcal. / protein 3,91g. fat:3,24g.
µg. - Ph:1,89 Na:0,11 Ka:4,29 Mg:0,99 Ca:0,53 Fe:0,05 Zn:0,02 Col.:0 Hsr.:0,77

Quantity of ingredients:
Millet 1 cup / 120g. (yes)
Water 1 1/2 cups / 200g. (yes)
Grape juice red 1 1/2 cups / 240g. (little)
Pear 4 pieces / 600g. (yes)
Ginger fresh 1/2 teaspoon / 2g. (yes)
Salt 1 pinch / 1g. (little)
Acerola fruit nectar or powder 1 teaspoon / 2g. (little)
Cocoa 1 pinch / 1g. (yes)
Sunflower seeds 2 table spoons / 4g. (yes)
Barley malt 1/2 teaspoon / 2g. (yes)
Cream, sweet 30% 2 teaspoons / 20g. (little)

Cooking instructions:
Simmer the millet for 5 min and let it swell for another 30 min.

Then: In a hot pot, heat some grape juice; add chopped pears, very little grated ginger, a pinch of salt, acerola, a pinch of cocoa and sauté briefly; add the boiled millet, sunflower seeds, some barley malt to taste, 1 tsp cream per
serving or a little butter.

9.29 Oyster mushrooms with asparagus

Forces, reduces inflammation, improves digestion, lowers cholesterol, strengthens kidney, stimulates liver function, improves blood circulation, improves medication effect, increases appetite.
Cooking time approx. 30 min
Allergens: GH
4 portions to 383g. / 316kcal. - (carb:50% / prot:50%)
100g.=82,64kcal. / protein 9,43g. fat:18,24g.
µg. - Ph:3,97 Na:0,3 Ka:15,49 Mg:1,21 Ca:1,51 Fe:0,05 Zn:0,03 Col.:0,39 Hsr.:7,1

Quantity of ingredients:
Onion white 1 piece / 50g. (yes)
Butter organic 2 table spoons / 40g. (little)
Oyster mushroom 3/4 lbs / 300g. (yes)
Sake 2 table spoons / 40g. (yes)
Parsley 2 table spoons / 40g. (yes)
Walnuts 3 table spoons / 60g. (yes)
Asparagus (green or white) 1,1 lbs / 500g. (yes)
Salt 1 pinch / 1g. (little)
Sugar white 1 pinch / 0,1g. (little)
Potato 1 lbs / 500g. (yes)
Salt (herbal) 1 pinch / 1g. (little)

Cooking instructions:
Cook organically grown potatoes with the skin, otherwise prepare peeled boiled potatoes. Boil the asparagus in salted water with a pinch of sugar and salt. (You can cook an old roll that absorbs the bittering substances.) Slightly sauté the chopped onions in a pan in the butter before frying the oyster mushrooms cut into the same pan. Stew 15 minutes, stirring several times. Add the sake, walnuts and parsley and simmer on low heat while you drain the potatoes and asparagus. Finally, sprinkle some herbal salt over it.
If no fresh asparagus is available, asparagus can be used in jars.

9.30 Paprika-tomato rice

Good to fight little cholesterol, diabetes. Low in protein, low fat content, little protein. Forcing spleen, dissolves stagnation, promotes weight loss. Good to fight immunodeficiency, loss of appetite, flatulence, high blood pressure, depressions.
Cooking time approx. 25 min
Allergens: L
3 portions to 324g. / 291kcal. - (carb:89% / prot:11%)
100g.=89,92kcal. / protein 7,63g. fat:2,54g.
µg. - Ph:10,3 Na:1,31 Ka:15,5 Mg:9,5 Ca:22,5 Fe:0,14 Zn:0,06 Col.:0 Hsr.:4,12

Quantity of ingredients:
Onion white 1 piece / 50g. (yes)
Peppers 4 pieces / 120g. (yes)
Bay leaf 2 pieces / 1g. (yes)
Clove 2 pieces / 1g. (yes)

Basic recipe for a vegetable soup (nutritious) 7/8 lbs / 400g. (yes)
Rice (whole grain) 5/8 oz / 200g. (yes)
Champignon 1/8 lbs - 2oz / 60g. (yes)
Parsley 1/2 oz / 20g. (yes)
Peppers (rose peppers) 1 pinch / 0,2g. (yes)
Tomato 1/4 lbs - 4oz / 120g. (yes)

Cooking instructions:
Finely chop the onion. Cut the peppers into fine strips.
Heat margarine in a saucepan, sauté onions and peppers, and rice.
Add the vegetable stock, add cloves and bay leaves and leave to
simmer in a closed pot for approx. 20 minutes. Cut the tomato meat into
1 cm cubes and add to the rice 5 minutes before the end of cooking.

9.31 Pasta with ham

Noodles protect the digestive organs. Tomato helps to digest fat. The
oils lower the cholesterol level. Chives strengthen gastric juice
production, promote digestion and blood circulation. Everything works
with loss of appetite.
Cooking time approx. 1 hour
Allergens: ACO
4 portions to 298,75g. / 839kcal. - (carb:38% / prot:62%)
100g.=280,84kcal. / protein 46,14g. fat:47,79g.
µg. - Ph:56,97 Na:22,13 Ka:59,3 Mg:8,46 Ca:40,55 Fe:0,33 Zn:0,45 Col.:37,16 Hsr.:20,59

Quantity of ingredients:
Noodles (wheat, ribbon noodles) with egg / 300g. (yes)
Pork ham cooked / 300g. (yes)
Chicken egg / 300g. (yes)
Olive oil / 20g. (yes)
Salt / 1g. (little)
Pepper (ground) / 0,5g. ()
Gouda cheese / 150g. (little)
Chives / 7g. (yes)
Tomato / 30g. (yes)
Sunflower seeds / 10g. (yes)
Sunflower oil / 30g. (yes)
Pumpkin seed oil / 15g. (yes)
Vinegar (Apple vinegar) / 15g. (yes)
Pear juice / 15g. (little)
Salt / 1g. (little)
Pepper (ground) / 0,5g. ()

Cooking instructions:
Cook the noodles in plenty of salted water until firm and drain well.
Cut the ham into 1 1/2 cm squares, heat the olive oil and fry the ham.
Put the noodles in a pan with a lid. Whisk the eggs with salt and pour over the noodles, put the lid on top and let it stand at low heat.
Cut the cheese into 1 cm wide strips, finely chop the chives. Cut tomatoes into small cubes.
Roast sunflowers in a coated pan.
Let the ready-made noodle pancake slide out of the pan and cut into fine strips.
Mix the pasta, ham, cheese, paprika and sunflower seeds.
From sunflower oil, pumpkin seed oil, apple cider vinegar, pear juice, salt and pepper stir a marinade and mix with the pasta.

9.32 Potato with dandelion salad

Promotes spleen, reduces inflammation, improves digestion, regenerates skin, supports urinating, lowers cholesterol, detoxifying, reduces inflammation, forcing spleen and digestive system, detoxifying, dissolves stagnation.
Cooking time approx. 25 min
2 portions to 203g. / 162kcal. - (carb:70% / prot:30%)
100g.=79,8kcal. / protein 4,28g. fat:5,59g.
µg. - Ph:26,58 Na:13,03 Ka:176,11 Mg:11,88 Ca:27,41 Fe:0,61 Zn:0,28 Col.:0,01
Hsr.:14,22

Quantity of ingredients:
Potato 5/8 lbs - 8oz / 250g. (yes)
Onion white 1/2 piece / 20g. (yes)
Sunflower oil 1 table spoon / 10g. (yes)
Dandelion (young plants) 1/4 lbs - 4oz / 125g. (yes)
Salt 1 pinch / 1g. (little)
Pepper white (ground) 1 pinch / 0,5g. (yes)

Cooking instructions:
Cook the potatoes in salted water and cut into thin slices. Finely chop the onion. Now season the potatoes with oil, salt and pepper and add the dandelion and mix.

9.33 Potato-basil soup

Reduces inflammation, improves digestion, supports urination, lowers cholesterol, reduces blood pressure, strengthens immune system, prevents cancer, reduces radiation damage, antioxidative, dissolves stagnation.
Cooking time approx. 25 min
Allergens: L
4 portions to 330g. / 96kcal. - (carb:69% / prot:31%)
100g.=28,94kcal. / protein 3,23g. fat:2,99g.
µg. - Ph:1,91 Na:3,35 Ka:13,03 Mg:0,61 Ca:2,91 Fe:0,03 Zn:0,01 Col.:0 Hsr.:1,9

Quantity of ingredients:
Water 2 cups / 450g. (yes)
Potato 4 pieces / 200g. (yes)
Carrot 2 pieces / 100g. (yes)
Celery root 1 piece / 500g. (yes)
Pepper (ground) 1 pinch / 0,5g. ()
Ground 1 pinch / 1g. (yes)
Garlic 1 clove / 3g. (yes)
Salt 1 pinch / 1g. (little)
Lemon 1 teaspoon / 3g. (yes)
Basil (fresh) 1 Bunch / 50g. (yes)
Peppers powder 1 pinch / 1g. (yes)
Sugar cane sugar 1 pinch / 1g. (little)
Olive oil 1 table spoon / 10g. (yes)

Cooking instructions:
Peeled and chopped 4 medium potatoes in a pot of hot water and 2 chopped medium carrots, a piece of celery root, a pinch of pepper, a pinch of ground cumin, crushed a small clove of garlic, a pinch of salt, 1 teaspoon of lemon juice, simmer until the Vegetables is soft.

Add 1 bunch finely chopped basil into one half of the soup and puree everything; stir in the other half of the basil; with rose paprika, a pinch of whole cane sugar, 1 tablespoon of olive oil or butter, freshly ground pepper, salt to taste.

9.34 Pumpkin curry

Promotes digestion and sweating, Dissolves stagnation, strengthens lungs and spleen, diuretic, reduces blood glucose, forcing spleen and digestive system, detoxifying, strengthens the muscles and bones.
Cooking time approx. 20 min
3 portions to 251g. / 193kcal. - (carb:63% / prot:37%)
100g.=77,03kcal. / protein 2,72g. fat:10,61g.
µg. - Ph:5,14 Na:0,86 Ka:16,34 Mg:2,68 Ca:2,29 Fe:0,06 Zn:0,02 Col.:0 Hsr.:1,54

Quantity of ingredients:
Pumpkin 3/4 lbs / 300g. (yes)
Olive oil 2 table spoons / 30g. (yes)
Coriander 1 pinch / 1g. (yes)
Pepper (ground) 1 pinch / 0,5g. ()
Curry 1 pinch / 1g. (yes)
Water 1/4 cup / 50g. (yes)
Salt 1 pinch / 1g. (little)
Parsley 1 table spoon / 7g. (yes)
Cardamom 1 pinch / 1g. (yes)
Turmeric (yellow root) 1 pinch / 1g. (yes)
Rice (whole grain) 1/2 cup / 60g. (yes)
Water 3 cups / 300g. (yes)
Salt 1 pinch / 1g. (little)

Cooking instructions:
Heat olive oil in pan. Steam the pumpkin cut in cubes, season with cilantro, pepper and curry, simmer with a little water, salt with sea salt, add chopped parsley with cardamom and turmeric, simmer on a small fire for about 10 minutes, depending on the pumpkin, the pumpkin should still be firm.

Place the rice in salted water, bring to the boil and let it simmer over low heat for about 15 minutes.

9.35 Pumpkin soup

Promotes digestion, forcing spleen and stomach, reduces blood pressure, strengthens immune system, prevents cancer, reduces radiation damage, improves digestion, regenerates skin, lowers cholesterol, reduces blood glucose, protects liver.
Cooking time approx. 1 hour
3 portions to 236,33g. / 105kcal. - (carb:71% / prot:29%)
100g.=44,29kcal. / protein 2,54g. fat:3,64g.
µg. - Ph:4,02 Na:0,96 Ka:24,72 Mg:1,82 Ca:2,89 Fe:0,08 Zn:0,02 Col.:0 Hsr.:1,08

Quantity of ingredients:
Pumpkin 3/4 lbs / 300g. (yes)
Carrot 2 pieces / 100g. (yes)
Potato 2 pieces / 120g. (yes)
Olive oil 1 table spoon / 10g. (yes)
Onion white 1 piece / 50g. (yes)
Water 1 cup / 120g. (yes)
Parsley 1 table spoon / 7g. (yes)
Anise (Common Fennel) 1 pinch / 1g. (yes)
Salt 1 pinch / 1g. (little)

Cooking instructions:
Add the olive oil to the pan, add the diced pumpkin, diced carrots and potatoes. Roast them shortly, add the finely chopped onion, fill with water, add enough water to cover the vegetables at least 3 finger-widths. Boil at low heat.

Season with sea salt, add small cutted parsley, a pinch of anise (little). Allow to simmer for about 35 minutes. Then purée the soup and add some water, depending on the consistency of
the soup.

9.36 Pumpkin-yoghurt soup

Relaxes, reduces blood pressure, strengthens immune system, promotes weight loss. Good to fight immunodeficiency, loss of appetite, flatulence, depressions, diabetes, diarrhea.
Cooking time approx. 15 min
Allergens: GL
4 portions to 239g. / 68kcal. - (carb:83% / prot:17%)
100g.=28,45kcal. / protein 2,37g. fat:1,31g.
µg. - Ph:1,79 Na:0,9 Ka:6,6 Mg:2,8 Ca:10,96 Fe:0,02 Zn:0,01 Col.:0,05 Hsr.:0,35

Quantity of ingredients:
Basic recipe for a vegetable soup (nutritious) 1 cup / 300g. (yes)
Hokkaido pumpkin 1,1 lbs / 500g. (yes)
Ginger fresh 1/2 teaspoon / 2g. (yes)
Fennel seeds ground 1/2 teaspoon / 1g. (yes)
Anise (Common Fennel) 1/4 teaspoon / 1g. (yes)
Yogurt (natural, 1.5% fat) 3/8 lbs - 6oz / 150g. (yes)
Peppermint 2 leaves / 1g. (yes)
Salt 1 pinch / 1g. (little)

Cooking instructions:
Heat the vegetable broth (after the basic recipe) till it boils. Add diced
pumpkin, chopped ginger, crushed fennel seeds and anise. Bring the
soup to the boil and simmer for about 12 minutes until the pumpkin is
soft.
Remove soup from the heat. Puree the soup with the yoghurt with the
blender. Serve soup with finely chopped mint sprinkled.

9.37 Refreshing cucumber soup with potatoes

Diuretic, detoxifying, suppresses conversion of sugar into fat, lowers
cholesterol, prevents cancer, reduces inflammation, improves digestion,
lowers cholesterol, dissolves stagnation, improves blood circulation,
stimulates appetite.
Cooking time approx. 15 min
Allergens: GN
3 portions to 307,33g. / 148kcal. - (carb:70% / prot:30%)
100g.=48,26kcal. / protein 3,93g. fat:5,09g.
µg. - Ph:3,72 Na:0,77 Ka:23,54 Mg:1,43 Ca:2 Fe:0,05 Zn:0,02 Col.:0 Hsr.:1,19

Quantity of ingredients:
Sesame oil 1 table spoon / 10g. (yes)
Potato 4 pieces / 300g. (yes)
Onion (spring onion) 3 pieces / 60g. (yes)
Pepper (ground) 1 pinch / 0,5g. ()
Nutmeg 1 pinch / 1g. (yes)
Salt 1 pinch / 1g. (little)
Lemon 1/2 piece / 25g. (yes)
Cucumber 2 pieces / 500g. (yes)
Cream, sweet 30% 1 table spoon / 10g. (little)
Dill 1 table spoon / 15g. (yes)

Cooking instructions:
Sauté sesame oil, chopped potatoes, plenty of spring onions in a hot pot; add pepper, a little nutmeg, salt, lemon juice, hot water, diced cucumber; simmer for about 10 minutes and then puree; add some sweet cream as you like,
and fresh dill.

Variation: Add a little chili, oregano, thyme or rosemary to soften the cooling effect.

9.38 Rice salad with mint

Strengthens stomach and spleen, promotes digestion, supports urination.
Peppermint relaxes, stimulates bile flow and bile juice production.
Paprika regulates hydrogen exchange, prevents heart disease.
Cooking time approx. 1 1/2 hours
4 portions to 304,75g. / 878kcal. - (carb:70% / prot:30%)
100g.=288,19kcal. / protein 15,96g. fat:35,18g.
µg. - Ph:41,49 Na:1,57 Ka:48,5 Mg:19,08 Ca:4,64 Fe:0,35 Zn:0,3 Col.:0,03 Hsr.:13,92

Quantity of ingredients:
Rice long grain rice / 300g. (yes)
Peas / 80g. (yes)
Onion (spring onion) / 50g. (yes)
Peppers / 300g. (yes)
Corn / 300g. (yes)
Peppermint / 15g. (yes)
Garlic / 5g. (yes)
Olive oil / 125g. (yes)
Salt / 1g. (little)
Pepper (ground) / 0,5g. ()
Lemon juice / 10g. (yes)
Sugar white / 3g. (little)
Water / 30g. (yes)

Cooking instructions:
For the rice salad, bring the water to a boil in a large saucepan and stir in the rice. Bring to a boil and simmer for 12-15 minutes until the rice is firm. Strain and allow to cool.
Cook the peas in a pot of boiling water for about 2 minutes. Then rinse under cold water and drain.
For the dressing, stir in oil, lemon juice, garlic and sugar in a small bowl. Season with salt and freshly ground black pepper.

Place rice, peas, green onions, red and green peppers, corn and mint in a large bowl. Add dressing and mix well. Cover and let cool for about 1 hour.
Serve in a salad bowl.

9.39 Roasted barley patties

Improves digestion, lowers cholesterol, good to fight diarrhea, ulceration, joint pain, stomach problems. Promotes spleen and liver, reduces blood pressure, strengthens immune system, prevents cancer, reduces radiation damage, stimulates liver function.
Cooking time approx. 1 1/2 hours
Allergens: ACN
3 portions to 292,67g. / 398kcal. - (carb:63% / prot:37%)
100g.=135,99kcal. / protein 8,38g. fat:19,69g.
µg. - Ph:7,07 Na:4,18 Ka:17,24 Mg:2,02 Ca:2,5 Fe:0,08 Zn:0,04 Col.:2,76 Hsr.:2,93

Quantity of ingredients:
Water 1 1/2 cups / 250g. (yes)
Barley grouts 1 cup / 120g. (yes)
Potato 1 piece / 140g. (yes)
Carrot 1 piece / 120g. (yes)
Champignon 2-3 pieces / 25g. (yes)
Chicken egg 1 piece / 55g. (yes)
Onion white 1 piece / 50g. (yes)
Ginger fresh 1/2 teaspoon / 1g. (yes)
Pepper (ground) 1 pinch / 0,5g. ()
Salt 1 pinch / 1g. (little)
Lemon 1/2 piece / 15g. (yes)
Parsley 2 table spoons / 15g. (yes)
Peppers powder 1 pinch / 1g. (yes)
Sesame oil 2 table spoons / 50g. (yes)
Bread roll 1 piece / 35g. (little)

Cooking instructions:
Preparation:
Place 2 large cups of hot water in a saucepan; add 1 large cup of barley porridge; simmer for 2 minutes while stirring; then let it swell for 20 minutes on the switched off stove; take down and let cool.
Cook in boiling water 1 large potato, chopped and cut.
Soak 1 roll in hot water and squeeze well.
Then: Mix the barley groats and crushed the potato. Add 1 grated carrot, 2 - 3 chopped mushrooms, 1 egg, 1 finely
chopped onion, 1/2 teaspoon grated ginger, a pinch of pepper, a pinch

of salt, a little lemon juice, chopped parsley, plenty of rose paprika; knead well and form patties; heat sesame oil in a hot pan; fry the patties for about 15 minutes over a gentle heat; turn at half time.

Also fits well: lettuce, soybean vegetables.

9.40 Rosemary Potatoes

Reduces Inflammation, improves digestion, regenerates skin, supports urination, lowers cholesterol. Rosemary stimulates digestion, strengthens lung, promotes spleen and kidney, dries out.
Cooking time approx. 30 min
2 portions to 216,5g. / 188kcal. - (carb:76% / prot:24%)
100g.=87,07kcal. / protein 4,21g. fat:5,25g.
µg. - Ph:11,51 Na:0,72 Ka:82,88 Mg:4,72 Ca:1,86 Fe:0,1 Zn:0,07 Col.:0 Hsr.:3,64

Quantity of ingredients:
Potato 6-8 pieces / 420g. (yes)
Salt (herbal) 1 pinch / 1g. (little)
Olive oil 1 table spoon / 10g. (yes)
Rosemary 1 teaspoon / 2g. (yes)

Cooking instructions:
Cut the potatoes into half´s, apply a little olive oil on the cut surface, then salt, sprinkle 2 - 3 rosemary needles on the potatoes.
Place the potatoes on the baking tray and bake them in the preheated oven for approx. 25 minutes to 190°C/374°F.

9.41 Semolina dumpling soup

Reduces blood pressure, strengthens immune system, prevents cancer, reduces radiation damage, dissolves stagnation, promotes weight loss. Good to fight immunodeficiency, loss of appetite, flatulence, high blood pressure, depressions, diabetes, diarrhea.
Cooking time approx. 1 hour
Allergens: ACGLO
3 portions to 235,67g. / 287kcal. - (carb:74% / prot:26%)
100g.=121,78kcal. / protein 12,68g. fat:16,24g.
µg. - Ph:7,29 Na:3,79 Ka:6,29 Mg:7,72 Ca:17,64 Fe:0,11 Zn:0,11 Col.:5,65 Hsr.:2,66

Quantity of ingredients:
Butter organic 1/8 lbs - 2oz / 40g. (little)
Chicken egg 1 piece / 65g. (yes)
Salt 1 pinch / 1g. (little)
Pepper (ground) 1 pinch / 0,5g. ()

Nutmeg 1 pinch / 1g. (yes)
Wheat semolina 3 oz / 80g. (yes)
Parsley 1 table spoon / 10g. (yes)
Chives 1 table spoon / 10g. (yes)

Cooking instructions:
Knead the ingredients for the dumplings to a firm dough and allow to swell for 30 minutes. Heat the broth (basic recipe for a beef broth warming). Then cut out with a spoon dumplings, place in the prepared broth and let stand for 20 minutes. Before serving, chop parsley and sprinkle with thinly sliced chives.

9.42 Semolina soup with vegetables

Reduces blood pressure, strengthens immune system, prevents cancer, forcing spleen, dissolves stagnation, promotes weight loss. Good to fight immunodeficiency, loss of appetite, flatulence, high blood pressure, depressions, diabetes, diarrhea, rheumatism, heartburn, twelffinger intestinal ulcers.
Cooking time approx. 20 min
Allergens: AGL
3 portions to 237,67g. / 105kcal. - (carb:85% / prot:15%)
100g.=44,32kcal. / protein 2,38g. fat:4,24g.
µg. - Ph:2,88 Na:3,04 Ka:8,54 Mg:9,5 Ca:37,49 Fe:0,11 Zn:0,03 Col.:0 Hsr.:1,7

Quantity of ingredients:
Basic recipe for a vegetable soup (nutritious) 2 cup / 500g. (yes)
Wheat semolina 2 table spoons / 20g. (yes)
Lovage 1/2 teaspoon / 2g. (yes)
Basil (fresh) 1/2 teaspoon / 1g. (yes)
Nutmeg 1 pinch / 0,1g. (yes)
Carrot 1/4 lbs - 4oz / 100g. (yes)
Celery root 1/8 lbs - 2oz / 50g. (yes)
Cream, sweet 30% 3 table spoons / 30g. (little)
Parsley 1 table spoon / 10g. (yes)

Cooking instructions:
Roast wheat grits without fat in a pan. Roast the chopped carrots and celery briefly. Add the vegetable soup (Basic recipe for a vegetable soup). Season with lovage, nutmeg and let it 10 min. simmer.
Stir in the cream before serving and garnish with parsley.

9.43 Spelled with fruit and nuts

Stops diarrhea, promotes digestion, appetizing, relieves fatigue, anti-inflammatory (gastrointestinal). Good to fight tumor lesions and leukemia, is antiallergic in food allergies, regulates metabolism, lowers blood glucose and cholesterol.
Cooking time approx. 1 1/2 hours
Allergens: AH
3 portions to 286,33g. / 290kcal. - (carb:76% / prot:24%)
100g.=101,16kcal. / protein 8,64g. fat:6,67g.
µg. - Ph:9,7 Na:8,81 Ka:25,53 Mg:3,53 Ca:2,83 Fe:0,14 Zn:0,02 Col.:0 Hsr.:2,96

Quantity of ingredients:
Spelled grain 1 cup / 120g. (yes)
Water 1 cup / 50g. (yes)
Apple (sweet) 1 piece / 220g. (little)
Apricot 1 piece / 200g. (yes)
Peaches 1 piece / 120g. (yes)
Cinnamon ground 1 pinch / 1g. (yes)
Cardamom 1 pinch / 1g. (yes)
Salt 1 pinch / 1g. (little)
Strawberries 1 cup / 120g. (yes)
Almond puree 1 table spoon / 15g. (yes)
Cocoa 1 pinch / 1g. (yes)
Walnuts 1 table spoon / 10g. (yes)

Cooking instructions:
Put spelled in hot water and cook.

Then: Give sweet chopped fruit (apples, apricots, peaches) in a little hot water, with a little cinnamon, sauté briefly; ground cardamom and / or coriander, a small pinch of salt, the boiled spelled, berries after season. Put some cocoa and roasted nuts over it.

9.44 Tea from cinnamon sticks

Antibacterial, good to fight vomiting, loss of appetite, flatulence, diabetes. Improves blood circulation, antipyretic, diuretic, cramp-dissolving, mucus-releasing, analgesic, diaphoretic, reduces the blood glucose level.
Cooking time approx. 15 min
1 portion to 126g. / 2kcal. - (carb:92% / prot:8%)
100g.=1,59kcal. / protein 0,04g. fat:0,03g.
µg. - Ph:0,48 Na:1,19 Ka:3,73 Mg:1,43 Ca:14,32 Fe:0,04 Zn:0,1 Col.:0 Hsr.:0

Quantity of ingredients:
Cinnamon sticks 1/4 piece / 1g. (yes)
Water 1 cup / 125g. (yes)

Cooking instructions:
A quarter of a cinnamon stick for a cup of tea. Start cold and bring to the boil. Let it sit for 15 minutes, then strain.
This tea is unsweetened and swallowed, slowly drunk. The amount is enough for one day.

9.45 Tea Green tea

Green tea promotes digestion, supports urination, dissolves mucus, detoxifying, stimulates nerves, reduces blood lipids, lowers cholesterol, reduces inflammation.
Cooking time approx. 10 min
1 portion to 122g. / 2kcal. - (carb:20% / prot:80%)
100g.=1,64kcal. / protein 0g. fat:0g.
µg. - Ph:5,61 Na:1,07 Ka:27,59 Mg:4,07 Ca:9,43 Fe:0,03 Zn:0,1 Col.:0 Hsr.:0

Quantity of ingredients:
Green tea 1 teaspoon / 2g. (yes)
Water 1 cup / 120g. (yes)

Cooking instructions:
For each cup you use a teaspoonful or a teabag.
Pour green tea only with 60 to 80 ° C / 140 to 176 °F hot water, otherwise it will be bitter.
If the tea has a stimulating effect, let it draw for two to three minutes. It has a calming effect for a duration of five minutes (no longer, otherwise it will be bitter!).
Another method: Pour the tea leaves with about 70 ° C / 158 °F hot water and pour the water immediately again. Then just pour hot water again. The bitter substances disappear and the tea gets a milder aroma.

9.46 Tea rooibos

Antioxidant, anti-inflammatory, anticancer, flavonoids, it also has a positive effect on Alzheimer, arteriosclerosis. Antiallergic, inhibits histamine release. Antibacterial, antiviral, antifungal, detoxifying (alkaline).
Cooking time approx. 10 min.
5 portions to 200,8g. / 0kcal. - (carb:0% / prot:0%)
100g.=0kcal. / protein 0g. fat:0g.
µg. - Ph:0 Na:0,2 Ka:0 Mg:0,2 Ca:1 Fe:0 Zn:0,02 Col.:0 Hsr.:0

Quantity of ingredients:
Rooibos tea 4 teaspoons / 4g. (rec.)
Water 4 cup / 1000g. (yes)

Cooking instructions:
Brew 3-4 teaspoons of rooibos with one liter of boiling water and leave for 6-10 minutes. With soft water you use less tea for the preparation, with harder water we recommend a higher dosage.

9.47 Vegetable semolina soup

Diuretic, harmonizes the stomach and intestines, conducts bowel winds, reduces blood pressure, lowers cholesterol, detoxifying, good to fight loss of appetite, flatulence, inflammatory bowel disease, heartburn, twelffinger intestinal ulcers. Stimulates digestion, reduces pain.
Cooking time approx. 20 min
Allergens: AEGL
3 portions to 459,67g. / 199kcal. - (carb:79% / prot:21%)
100g.=43,22kcal. / protein 6,38g. fat:7,02g.
µg. - Ph:4,26 Na:4,63 Ka:23,27 Mg:6,33 Ca:22,08 Fe:0,09 Zn:0,04 Col.:0,39 Hsr.:2,88

Quantity of ingredients:
Basic recipe for a vegetable soup (nutritious) 2 cup / 500g. (yes)
Potato 1 piece / 80g. (yes)
Parsnip 1 piece / 180g. (yes)
Carrot 1 piece / 120g. (yes)
Celery root 3/8 lbs - 6oz / 150g. (yes)
Kohlrabi 1/2 piece / 200g. (yes)
Beans (green, fresh) 1/4 lbs / 100g. (yes)
Wheat semolina 2 table spoons / 24g. (yes)
Lovage 1/2 teaspoon / 2g. (yes)
Butter organic 1 table spoon / 20g. (little)
Soy sauce 1 teaspoon / 3g. (yes)

Cooking instructions:
Worm the prepared vegetable soup; cook the vegetables in the soup softly. Spread some wheatgrass and let it swell. At the end, add lovage-green and a little butter and taste with soy sauce.

10 Effects of food

10.1 Use ingredients: recommendable

Acai powder
Bitter Herb liqueur
Fox nut, gorgon nut, makhana

Hibiscus
Kudzu
Lily bulbs

10.2 Use ingredients: yes

Adzuki beans
Agar agar (kelp)
Agrimony
Almond
Almond milk
Almond puree
Amaranth
Amaranth Pops
Anchovy / Sardine
Angelica root
Anise (Common Fennel)
Apple (sour)
Apricot
Arrowroot
Artichoke
Asparagus (green or white)
Aubergine
Avocado
Baking powder
Balm
Bamboo shoots
Banchatee (green tea)
barberry
Barley
Barley flour
Barley grass powder
Barley grouts
Barley malt
Barley not peeled
Basic recipe for a beef soup
Basic recipe for a beef soup (warming)
Basic recipe for a chicken soup
(warming)
Basic recipe for a duck soup
Basic recipe for a fish soup
Basic recipe for a rice soup (Congee)
Basic recipe for a vegetable soup
(nutritious)
Basil
Basil (fresh)
Batavia
Bay leaf
Bean oil

Beans (green, fresh)
Bearberry leaf
Beef fillet
Beef lungs (calf)
Beef meat
Beef meat (calf)
Beef meatbones
Berries of the season
Bitter orange peel
Black beans
Black caraway
Black fungus mushroom
Black tea
Blackberry dried (unripe fruit)
Blackberry leaves
Blackberry´s
Black-eyed peas
Blackthorn (Sloe)
Blue mallow tee
Blueberry
Bocksdorn fruits (Fructus Lycii, Goji,
goji berry dried
Boletus mushroom
Borage
Borage oil
Boxhorn clover seeds
Brazil nuts
Bread with carob kernel flour
Breadcrumbs (wheat bread, bread roll)
Brie cheese
Broad beans (thick beans)
Broccoli
Brussels sprouts
Buckbean
Buckwheat
Buckwheat (roasted) Kasha
Buckwheat whole grain
Bulgur (cereals)
Burdock root tea
Bush beans
Butter (half fat)
Butter beans white
Buttermilk

Calamari
Camembert
Campari
Cantaloupe
Capers in olive oil
Carambola (Star fruit)
Cardamom
Carob flour, St. john's bread
Carp
Carrot
Carrot (Early Carrot)
Carrot juice without sugar
Cashews
Cauliflower
Caviar
Celery root
Celery sticks
Cereal coffee
Chamomile
Chamomile tea
Champignon
Channa-Dal
Chanterelle
Chenpi (chinese tangerine bowl)
Cherry
Cherry (sour)
Chervil
Chervil dried
Chestnut puree
Chestnuts
Chicken Blood
Chicken egg
Chicken egg white
Chicken meat
Chicken yolk
Chickpeas
Chickweed
Chicory
Chili (pod or ground)
Chinese cabbage
Chinese pearl barley
Chives
Chlorella (fresh water)
Chrysanthemum blossom tea
Cinnamon ground
Cinnamon sticks
Clementine
Clementines
Clove
Cocoa
Coconut flakes
Coconut grated
Coconut meat
Coconut milk

Cod
Codfish
Coffee
Coix (seeds) YiYi Ren
Cola drink (low calorie)
Cooking oil
Coriander
Coriander (fresh)
Corn
Corn (fast polenta)
Corn (roasted)
Corn flour
Corn germ oil
Corn Grease (Polenta)
Corn silk tea
Corn starch
Cottage cheese
Couscous
Cow's milk (1.5% fat)
Crab
Cranberries
Cranberry
Cranberry
Cranberry juice
Cream sour 10%
Creamer
Cress
Crispbread
Crucian
Cucumber
Cucumber (bitter)
Cucumber (spicy cucumber)
Cumin (Caraway seed)
Curcuma
Curd cheese 20%
Currant (black)
Currant (red)
Currant (white)
Curry
Curry paste red
Daisy
Dandelion (young plants)
Dandelion juice
Dandelionroots tea
Dashi
Dates red
Deer meat
Deer meat
Deer's Bones
Dill
Dulse (seaweed)
Dyer's broom herb
Edam cheese
Elderberries

Elderberry blossom tee
Endive salad
Evening primrose oil
Fennel
Fennel seeds ground
Fennel tea
Fenugreek (Trigonella foenum-graecum)
Fernet Branca (herbal bitter liqueur)
Feta cheese
Feta cheese
Fig
Fish innards
Fish pieces mixed (fresh water)
Fish remains
Fish sauce
Flounder
Flower pollen
French beans
Fresh cheese
Fresh cheese from soya
Fresh cheese with herbs
Freshwater crab
Freshwater fish
Fruit tea
Gail plum
Galangal
Garam Masala powder
Garlic
Gelatin white
Gelee Royal
Gentian root
Gentian root tea
Ginger fresh
Ginger oil
Ginger powder
Ginkgo fruit
Ginseng
Ginseng root
Goat
Goat and sheep's blood
Goat and sheep's milk
Goat cheese
Goose blood
Goose egg
Gooseberry
Gouda cheese
Gourd
Grapefruit (Pomelo)
Grapefruit dried peel
Grapefruit juice
Grapeseed oil
Grass carp
Green spelt

Green tea
Greengage
Ground
Ground caraway
Guava
Halibut (Flatfish)
Hawthorn
Hazelnuts
Herbal tea mix
Herbs bitter
Herbs of Provence
Herbs various
Herbs wild
Herring
Hibiscus tea
Hijiki
Hokkaido pumpkin
Hop
Horehound leaves
Horse meat
Hyssop
Iceberg lettuce
Jasmine blossoms tee
Jellyfish
Juniper berry
Kaki plum
Kalmus
Kefir
Kidney beans (red)
King Solomon's-seal
Kiwi
Kohlrabi
Kombu seaweed (Saccharina japonica)
Kukicha tea
Kumquats
Lamb bones
Lamb meat
Lamb shoulder
Lamb's lettuce
Lamb's lettuce
Lavender blossoms
Leaf salads (bitter)
Leek
Lemon
Lemon Balm (dried)
Lemon Balm (fresh)
Lemon juice
Lemon peel
Lemongrass
Lentils
Lentils black
Lentils red
Lentils yellow
Lettuce

Licorice root tea
Lima beans
Lime
Lime blossom tea
Linseed
Linseed (crushed)
Linseed oil
Liver smoothing tea
Lobster
Longane
Loquate / Japanese medlar
Lotus roots
Lotus seeds
Lovage
Lovage seeds
Luo Han Guo fruit
Lychee
Lychee in Preserved
Mackerel
Mallow (Malva sylvestris) blossom tea
Malt
Mango
Manioc flour
Mare's milk
Margarine
Marjoram
Martini
Mayonnaise 80%
Mediterranean fish (cod, plaice, haddock, sea eel, mackerel)
Medlar
Millet
Millet flakes
Mineral water
Mirabelle plum
Miso
Miso black (fermented)
Miso paste (soy bean paste)
Mixed Pickles
Mold cheese
Morel (black, dried)
Morel, dried
Mozzarella
Mu Erh Mushroom
Muesli
Mulled Wine Spice
Mullet
Multi-grain bread (gray bread)
Mung bean
Mung bean sprouting
Mussels
Mustard
Mustard Dijon
Mustard medium hot

Mustard seeds
Mustard sweet
Mutton
Mutton
Nasturtium (nose-twister or nose-tweaker)
Nectarine
Nettles
Noodles (wheat) with egg
Noodles (wheat, lasagne) with egg
Noodles (wheat, ribbon noodles) with egg
Noodles (wheat, spaghetti) with egg
Noodles (whole grain) with egg
Nori, purple seaweed, red algae
Nutmeg
Oat
Oat flakes (whole grain)
Oat flakes roasted
Oat flour
Oat fusion (baby food)
Oat meal
Oat milk
Octopus
Octopus
Okra
Olive oil
Olives
Olives green
Onion (shallot)
Onion (spring onion)
Onion read
Onion white
Orange
Orange blossom
Orange dried peel
Orange grated peel
Orange peel
Oregano dried
Oregano fresh
Oyster mushroom
Oyster shell powder
Oysters
Palm oil
Papaya
Parsley
Parsley root
Parsnip
Passion blossoms tea
Passion fruit
Peaches
Peaches (canned)
Peanut oil
Peanuts

Pear
Pearl barley
Pearl barley
Peas
Peas, green
Pepper (ground)
Pepper Cayenne
Pepper powder (hot)
Pepper white (ground)
Peppercorns
Peppermint
Peppermint tea
Pepperoni
Pepperoni, red, pitted, halved
Pepperoni, yellow, pitted, halved
Peppers
Peppers (rose peppers)
Peppers (sweet)
Peppers powder
Perch
Pheasant
Pickle
Pig blood
Pigeon
Pigeon egg
Pimento
Pine nuts
Pineapple
Pineapple juice without sugar
Pinto beans speckled
Pistachios
Plaice
Plum
Plums
Pomegranate
Poppy
Pork ham
Pork ham cooked
Pork ham smoked
Pork knuckle
Pork lung
Pork meat
Pork skin
Potato
Potato (mealy)
Potato flour
Prickly pear
Processed cheese 12%
Psyllium seed
Pudding powder vanilla
Pumpernickel (dark bread)
Pumpkin
Pumpkin seed oil
Pumpkin seeds

Quince
Quinoa
Rabbit
Rabbit (wild)
Rabbit meat
Radicchio
Radish
Radish (white, green, purple-red)
Radish black
Radish horseradish
Radish leaves
Rapeseed oil
Raspberry
Raspberry leaf tea
Red beet
Red berry (without sugar)
Red wine
Reishi mushroom
Rhubarb
Ribworttea
Rice (fragrance)
Rice (Gaoliang / Sorghum)
Rice (whole grain)
Rice Basmati
Rice black
Rice flour
Rice long grain rice
Rice malt
Rice mash
Rice noodles
Rice red
Rice round grain
Rice starch
Rice sticky
Rice variety any
Rice wild (nature rice)
Romaine lettuce / lettuce salad
Rose blossom tea
Rose hip
Rose hip tea
Rose leaf tea
Rosefish
Rosemary
Rucola
Rusk
Rye
Rye flour
Rye wholemeal bread
Safflower (Dyer's thistle / Hong Hua)
Saffron
Sage
Sago (cereals)
Sake
Salmon

Salsify
Sauerkraut (cutted cabbage fermented)
Savory
Savoy cabbage / kale
Sea buckthorn
Sea cucumber
Seacrab
Sesame oil
Sesame oil roasted
Sesame paste (Tahini)
Sesame, black
Sesame, white
Shark
Sheep's milk
Sheep's milk yoghurt
Shiitake, dried
Shrimp
Shrimps
Skim milk powder
Slug
Sorrel
Sour cherries
Sour milk
Sour milk cheese 20%
Sourdough
Soy flour
Soy noodles
Soy sauce
Soy Tofu
Soy Tofu smoked
Soya Cuisine (soy cream)
Soybean milk
Soybean oil
Soybeans
Soybeans, black
Soybeans, blacks, fermented
Soybeans, yellow
Spelled (Dark) bread
Spelled flakes
Spelled grain
Spelled semolina
Spelled wholemeal flour
Spinach
Spiny lobsters
Spurdog (spiny dogfish, Schillerlocken)
St. Benedict's thistle, blessed thistle,
holy thistle, spotted thistle
Star anise
Stevia (candyleaf, sweetleaf)
Strawberries
Sugar fructose - fruit sugar
Sugar glucose - grapes sugar
Sugar Milk Sugar
Sugar substitute (sweetener)

Sunflower oil
Sunflower seeds
Sweet potato
Tabasco
Tangerine
Tarragon (Estragon)
Tea mixture uric acid lowering
Thistle oil
Thyme
Thyme dried
Toast bread (whole grain)
Tomato
Tomato dried
Tomato paste
Topinambur
Trout
Trout (smoked)
Truffle
Tsampa (roasted barley flour)
Tuna
Turkey breast meat
Turkey ham
Turmeric (yellow root)
Turnip
Turnips
Umeboshi paste
Umeboshi plums (Japanese apricots)
Valerian
Vanilla
Vanilla pod
Vanilla powder
Vegetable juice
Vinegar (Apple vinegar)
Vinegar (Red wine vinegar)
Vinegar Aceto Balsamico
Vinegar Aceto Balsamico white
Wakame
Walnut oil
Walnuts
Water
Water hot
Watermelon
Wax gourd
Wheat
Wheat bran
Wheat bulgur
Wheat flatbread/pita bread
Wheat flour
Wheat flour whole grain
Wheat germ oil
Wheat semolina
Wheat semolina for children
Wheat/Rye/Gray-black bread with yeast
Wheatgrass juice

Wheatgrass powder
Whey
White beans
White cabbage
Whitefish
Whole grain bread
Wholemeal flour
Wild boar meat
Wild garlic (garlic spinach)
Wild herbs
Wild strawberries

Wormwood herb
Yam root, yam root tuber
Yarrow
Yarrow tea
Yeast
Yew nut
Yoghurt vanilla
Yogi tea
Yogurt (natural, 1.5% fat)
Zucchini

10.3 Use ingredients: little

Acerola fruit nectar or powder
Agave nectar
Almond marzipan
Aloe juice
Apple (sweet)
Apple juice (natural cloudy)
Apple puree
Apricot dried
Apricot jam
Apricot nectar
Apricots
Apricots juice
Banana
Banana (cooking banana)
Beef bone marrow
Beef heart
Beef heart (calf)
Beef kidney
Beef liver
Beef Oxtail pieces
Beef soup meat
Beef stomach
Beer (alcohol-free)
Beer (alcohol-reduced)
Beer (Pils)
Beer (Top-fermented German dark beer)
Berry juice
Bitter Lemon
Bitter liqueur
Blackberry jam
Blueberry dried
Blueberry jam
Blueberry juice
Bread roll
Brown ale
Butter organic
Chard
Cherry compote

Cherry juice
Chicken heart
Chicken liver
Chicken stomach
Chocolate
Chocolate (Diabetic)
Clarified butter
Coconut fat
Cola drink
Compote (fruits of the season)
Cow's milk (whole milk 3.5% fat)
Cranberry jam
Cream (30% fat)
Cream sour 20%
Cream sour 30%
Cream, sweet 30%
Créme fraiche cheese
Curd cheese 40%
Currant jam (black)
Currant jam (red)
Currant juice (black)
Currants (black)
Currants (red)
Dates dried
Deer's kidneys
Duck (heart)
Duck (slaughtered)
Ducks egg
Eel
Eel smoked
Emmental cheese
Fig dried
Fructose (glucose)
Fruit mix juice
Ginseng liqueur
Goat and sheep's brain
Goat and sheep's liver
Goat and sheep's stomach
Goose

Goose fat
Goose parts
Gorgonzola
Grape juice red
Grape juice white
Grapes red
Grapes white
Honey
Honey wine (Met)
Ladyfingers
Lamb kidneys
Lamb liver
Lychee liqueur
Lye roll
Mango juice
Maple syrup
Mayonnaise 50%
Mulberry fruit
Orange jam
Orange juice
Parmesan
Peanut (roasted)
Peanut butter
Pear juice
Plum dried
Pork Bacon
Pork brain
Pork fat (lard)
Pork heart
Pork kidneys
Pork Lard
Pork liver
Pork marrow bones
Pork sausage (Bratwurst)
Pork stomach
Pork/beef sausage (smoked)
Pork's intestine
processed cheese 30%
Prosecco
Puff pastry

Quail
Quail egg
Rabbit liver
Raisins
Raspberry dried (immature)
Raspberry jam
Red cabbage
Rice sweet
Rum
Salt
Salt (herbal)
Sherry (whine)
Sour cream 15% fat
Spirit
Strawberry jam
Strawberry Juice
Sugar - icing sugar
Sugar brown
Sugar candy white
Sugar cane sugar
Sugar molasses
Sugar palm sugar
Sugar white
Tomato juice
Tomato puree
Tonic Water
Vanilla sugar natural
Walnuts roasted
Wheat beer
Wheat flakes
White bread (baguette)
White bread (pretzel sticks)
White bread (roll)
White bread (wheat bread)
White breadcrumbs
White dumpling bread (wheat bread cut into chunks)
White wine
Wormwood
Yogurt (natural, 3.5% fat)

10.4 Do not use contra-acting foods

Pineapple (from a can)   Supplementary nutrition

11 Complementary

11.1 Candyleaf, sweetleaf, sugarleaf

Stevia rebaudiana
Preparation: Cooking addition
Sweetener for diabetics or for weight loss. Hypotensive, antimicrobial, vasodilator effect.
Attention - consult with your doctor or therapist.
Dosage: As sweetener, dried or fresh
Some studies have described teratogenic and mutagenic effects in hamsters and rats, as well as mutagenicity in vitro. Not authorized in the EU as food. Stevia supporters see behind it a conspiracy of sugar lobby and bias of the European Commission. Finally, stevioside has been used in Asia for decades as a sweetener - so far without negative consequences.
Notice: The WHO studies on the effects of steviol in vivo have not shown any evidence of mutagenic effects in humans. Only at your own risk.

11.2 Fenugreek

Trigonellea foenumgraecum
Preparation: Cooking addition
Gives energy and strengthens.
Dosage: Active ingredients: Muzzilago, steroid saponins, sterols, flavonoids, high mucus content, proteins, fats

For seasoning always use as a powder, suitable in soups, stews, legumes, chicken, as a tea
Use the seeds only for germination: by briefly germinating the ingredients are potentiated and promote the digestion very extraordinary. For seasoning, they must first be roasted and then mortared.
as a tonic on senility: 1 tsp powder with water or warm milk, 1 cup daily (Ayurveda)
Notice: Do not use in pregnancy, yin-deficiency with heat, with infectious diseases.

11.3 Nettle leaves

Herba Urticae
Preparation: Healing tea (infusion)
Appetizing, Purifying, Hemostatic, Diarrhea, promotes blood formation,
Promotes hair growth, Diuretic, Urinary tract disorders,
 Rheumatism, Expectorant, Metabolism, Rheumatism, Arthritis,
Hypoglycemic, Detoxifying.
Dosage: Add 2-4 teaspoons of the tea to 250 ml of boiling water and
infuse for 10 minutes. Then sieve. Drink 2 to 3 cups per day as needed.
Active Ingredients: Flavonoids, Chlorophylls, Vitamins, Mineral Salts,
Beta-Sistosterol, Plant Acid, Histamine in the Hair,

11.4 Rooibos

Aspalathus linearis
Preparation: Healing tea (infusion)
Antioxidant, anti-inflammatory, anti-cancer, protects against flavanoids,
also has a positive effect on Alzheimer's, arteriosclerosis. Antiallergic,
inhibits histamine release. Antibacterial, antiviral, antifungal, detoxifying
(alkaline).
Dosage: Brew 3-4 teaspoons of rooibos with one liter of boiling water and
leave for 6-10 minutes. With soft water you need less tea for the
preparation, with harder water we recommend a higher dosage.

12 Basics of Nutrition

The basic principles of nutrition described herein are general recommendations. They are not aimed at a specific form of therapy. Recommendations concerning a therapy have priority.

12.1 Nutrition

Regular meals in a relaxed atmosphere. A warm breakfast is considered a good start into the day.
The main meals ought to be taken for lunch – supper in the early evening. Pay attention to feeling hungry or sated: don't eat too much nor remain hungry is the rule
Prepare the meals freshly from natural, regional products. Frozen, heat-conserved, industrially prepared or foodstuffs cooked in the microwave oven are rejected.
Choice of foodstuffs according to the season: more cooling food in summer, more warming food in winter.
Eat cooked food at least twice a day. Food and drinks ought to be lukewarm, never ice-cold or hot.
Raw vegetables, briefly cooked vegetables, freshly squeezed juices and mineral water are not recommended. Milk and dairy products are only included in the diet if they don't cause problems.
Don't use therapeutic recipes over a longer period without consulting your doctor or therapist.

Varied food
Enjoy the diversity of foodstuffs. Characteristics of a balanced nutrition are variety, suitable combination and a balanced quantity of rich and low energy foodstuffs (on one hand avoiding undersupply with essential nutrients and on the other hand to take to many undesirable substances).

A lot of Cereal Products - and Potatoes
Bread, pasta, rice, cereal flakes (best wholemeal) as well as potatoes contain almost no fat, but many vitamins, mineral nutrients, trace elements, roughage and secondary plant substances. These foodstuffs ought to be taken with low-fat side dishes.

Vegetables and Fruit – „Take Five" every day ...
5 portions of vegetables and fruit a day, as fresh as possible, briefly cooked, or maybe one portion as a juice – ideal as a side dish to every meal as well as snack between meals: Thus a lot of vitamins, mineral nutrients as well as roughage and secondary plant substances

Daily milk and dairy products
Milk and Dairy Products every Day, once or twice per Week Fish; meat, sausages as well as eggs moderately. These foodstuffs contain valuable nutrients like calcium in the milk, iodine selenium and omega-3 fat acids in saltwater fish. Meat is favorable due to its high content of disposable iron and the vitamins B1, B6 and B12. Quantities of 300 – 600 g meat and sausage per week are sufficient. Prefer low-fat products, especially in meat- and dairy products.

Low-fat and fatty Foodstuffs
Fat supplies us with essential fat acids and fatty foodstuffs contain also fat-soluble vitamins. Fat is high in energy; therefore much fat in the food may cause overweight, possibly also cancer. Too many saturated fat acids may further a tendency for cardio-vascular diseases in the long term. Prefer vegetable oils and fats (e.g. rapeseed-, olive-, soya-oils and solid fats produced therefrom). Beware of invisible fat in meat- and dairy products, pastry and sweets as well as in fast-food and convenience foods. 70 – 90 g fat per day is sufficient.

Moderately Sugar and Salt
Take sugar and foods/drinks containing various kinds of sugar (e.g. glucose syrup) only occasionally. Use herbs and spices as well as a little salt creatively. Prefer salt containing iodine.

Plenty of Liquids
Water is absolutely essential. Drink 1-2 l liquids every day. Prefer water (with or without gas) and other low-calorie drinks. Alcoholic drinks should not be taken.

Tasty Dishes, carefully cooked
Cook the meals with as low temperatures and as short as possible, using little water and fat – this preserves the original taste, keeps the nutrients intact and prevents the production of harmful compounds.

Take time and enjoy the food
Take your Time and enjoy your Food
Eating consciously helps to eat right. The eye enjoys food, too. It's fun, invites to enjoy varied dishes and stimulates the feeling of satiety.

Watch your Weight and stay in Motion
A balanced diet and a lot of exercise and sport (30 – 60 min/day) are a healthy combination. The right weight furthers well-being and health. Thermals, directional effectiveness, digestive power

There are various criteria for judging the effectiveness of herbs and foodstuffs.

The use of certain herbs and ingredients is based on observations of the effects on the body which these foodstuffs, herbs and spices show after having eaten them. The medical science has developed following system: Every ingredient or herb has a directional effectiveness. Furthermore, there are herbs which have a special effect on certain organs.

The basic condition for a healthy metabolism is to obtain sufficient energy from food and that the digestive process doesn't use too much energy. An easily digestible meal makes content and sated, doesn't cause flatulence and fatigue after the meal. The perfect spices increase the healthiness of our meals. Very often, just small doses of herbs and spices will suffice. They are not used to make us sated, but to help our digestive organs to digest the food.

12.2 Recipes

The recipes list the ingredients to be used and the cooking instructions show how the dish is prepared. The list of ingredients shows the concerned quantities as well as the relevance for the therapy. If you find „less than mentioned", try to comply or find an alternative from the „list of recommended foodstuffs". Mostly it shall result just in a small change of taste when you simply avoid this ingredient.

Mild cooking methods: boiling, stewing, poaching, steaming
Strong cooking methods: barbecuing, roasting, frying, smoking
Balanced cooking methods: deep-frying, baking brick
Deep-freezing and warming in the microwave oven should be avoided (denaturalization).

12.3 Foodstuffs

Foodstuffs have an effect on body and soul like medicinal herbs, only a very much milder one. Dietary advice is mainly based on regional foodstuffs. The knowledge about the effects of each foodstuff and the knowledge, when which foodstuff shall be used, is based on the orthodoschool of medicine. Use ecologic-organic products, if possible. As everything should be cooked for a long time due to a better digestability and very rarely eaten raw, the food agrees with everyone.

The classification of the foodstuffs according to their effect on the body is the basis in order to achieve a harmonious status of health.

Dietary advisors do not recommend certain foodstuffs for everyone. The individual diet is tailor-made for the individual constitution.

Buy only fresh and ripe fruit and vegetables. You ought to leave unripe fruit and vegetables and such with brown spots and wilted leaves behind in the market. In this case take deep-frozen goods (never ready-to-serve dishes!). Fruit and vegetables are deep-frozen immediately after harvesting and often contain more vitamins and minerals than the goods from the vegetable shelf. Whereas conserved or tinned goods contain very much less biological substances. Also, salt, sugar and others are mostly added to the latter. Never leave the foodstuffs in the water after washing them to avoid that many vital substances get drowned. Clean salads, fruit and vegetables immediately before serving.

Please make sure of the hygienic processing of foodstuffs. Clean your salads, fruit and vegetables carefully. When cooking with meat, prepare all ingredients first and then process the meat products. Clean the worktop and tools very carefully. Wooden surfaces ought to be treated with a mild disinfectant regularly in order to reduce germination.

Store fruit and vegetables separately, if possible. Harvested fruit and vegetables are still alive and emit e.g. ethylene gas, which makes other products ripen and age faster. Keep meat and fish in the closed packaging or store them in the fridge in closed containers.

12.4 Herbs

There are some basic rules for storing medicinal herbs. On principle, herbs must be protected from direct sunlight, humidity and heat.

Containers for the storage of herbs may be glasses, ceramic jars and even plastic containers. However, plastic is a rather unsuitable material and should only be a short-term solution. In case of glass containers, use a dark material.

Medicinal herbs cannot be kept for any long period. The shelf life of herbs is limited. However, it can be prolonged with suitable storage. The place should be dark, rather cool and absolutely dry. A wooden medicine cabinet, placed not directly next to a source of heat, would be ideal. Never buy large quantities of herbs so as not to have to throw them away. Label the container with the name of the herb and the date of harvesting or processing.

13 Other dietic-books

The following syndromes of dietetics, TCM or for a therapy supplement for cancer are available.

Dietetics

E001. Nutrition of the infant - baby food
E002. Nutrition during lactation
E003. Nutrition in old age
E004. Nutrition of children and adolescents
E005. Nutrition of athletes
E006. Light weight
E007. Pregnancy
E008. Full food

Protein and electrolyte - kidneys
E009. (hemodialysis) dialysis treatment
E010. Acute renal failure
E011. Chronic renal insufficiency
E012. Nephrotic syndrome
E013. Kidney stones (nephrolithiasis)

Gastrointestinal tract - pancreas
E014. Acute pancreatitis (inflammation of the pancreas)
E015. Chronic pancreatitis (inflammation of the pancreas)

Gastrointestinal tract - small intestine and large intestine
E016. Acute obstipation (constipation)
E017. Chronic obstipation (constipation)
E018. Colon irritabile
E019. Diverticulitis
E020. Acquired lactose intolerance (lactose malabsorption)
E021. Fructose malabsorption
E022. Glutensensitive enteropathy (celiac disease)
E023. Colectomy
E024. Short Bowel Syndrome

Gastrointestinal tract - liver, gallbladder, bile ducts
E025. Acute and chronic hepatitis (inflammation of the liver)
E026. Cholelithiasis (bile stones)
E027. fatty liver
E028. cirrhosis

Gastrointestinal tract - Stomach and duodenal intestine
E029. Acute gastritis
E030. Chronic gastritis
E031. Stomach bleeding
E032. Ulcus ventriculi and duodenal ulcer
E033. Condition after gastric surgery

Gastrointestinal tract - oral cavity and esophagus
E034. Stomatitis
E035. Esophageal carcinoma (esophageal cancer)
E036. Refluosophagitis (heartburn)

Special diseases
E037. Phenylketonuria (PKU)
E038. Rheumatic joint diseases

Metabolism
E039. Obesity (overweight)
E040. Diabetes mellitus
E041. Eating disorders (underweight)

Fat metabolism
E042. Hypercholesterolaemia (increased cholesterol level)
E043. Hepatic Encephalopathy

Heart and circulation
E044. Arteriosclerosis (arterial calcification)
E045. Heart insufficiency
E046. Hypertension
E047. Hyperuricaemia and gout

Changed nutrient requirements
E048. In case of fever
E049. For malignant diseases
E050. After burns
E051. Radiation and chemotherapy

CANCER
E100. Pancreatic cancer
E101. Bladder cancer
E102. Blood cancer (leukemia)
E103. Breast cancer
E104. Colorectal cancer
E105. Gastric cancer
E106. Kidney cancer
E107. Esophageal cancer

TCM
E200. Bladder - moisture heat in the bladder
E201. Bladder - moisture and cold in the bladder
E202. Bladder - emptiness and cold in the bladder
E203. Large intestine - external cold affects the large intestine
E204. Large intestine - moisture heat in the large intestine
E205. Large intestine - heat blocks the intestine II acute
E206. Large intestine - dryness of the colon
E207. Large intestine - Yang deficiency (cold)
E208. Heart - Blood insufficiency
E209. Heart - Blood stagnation
E210. Heart - Fire
E211. Heart - Hot mucus clogs the heart pores

E212. Heart - Cold mucus clogs the heart pores
E213. Heart - Qi deficiency
E214. Heart - Yang deficiency
E215. Heart - Yin deficiency
E216. Liver - Ascending Liver Yang
E217. Liver - Blood deficiency
E218. Liver - Blood stagnation
E219. Liver - Moisture heat in liver and gall bladder
E220. Liver - Fire
E221. Liver - Gall bladder Qi-Empty
E222. Liver - Cold in the liver meridian
E223. Liver - Qi stagnation
E224. Liver - Wind
E225. Liver - Wind with ascending liver Yang
E226. Liver - Wind with blood anemic
E227. Liver - Wind with extreme heat
E228. Lung - Qi deficiency
E229. Lung - Mucus-moisture in the lungs
E230. Lung - Mucus-heat in the lungs
E231. Lung - Mucus-cold in the lungs
E232. Lung - Dryness of the lungs
E233. Lung - Wind-heat attacks the lungs
E234. Lung - Wind-cold affects the lungs
E235. Lung - Yin deficiency
E236. Stomach - Bloodstagnation
E237. Stomach - Fire
E238. Stomach - Cold with liquid
E239. Stomach - Nutrition stagnation
E240. Stomach - Qi deficiency
E241. Stomach - Rebellious Qi
E242. Stomach - Yin Emptiness
E243. Spleen - Heat and moisture attack the spleen
E244. Spleen - Coldness and moisture affects the spleen
E245. Spleen - Qi deficiency
E246. Spleen - Qi deficiency + Declining spleen Qi
E247. Spleen - Qi deficiency + spleen does not control the blood
E248. Spleen - Yang deficiency
E249. Kidney - Heart and kidney no longer communicate
E250. Kidney - Jing deficiency
E251. Kidney - Kidneys cannot receive the Qi
E252. Kidney - Qi is not stable
E253. Kidney - Yang deficiency
E254. Kidney - Yin deficiency

For further information visit di-book.com.

14 EBNS - Software for nutritional counseling

The main task of the database is to create personalized nutritional advice for each patient individually. The database was developed for Dietetics and Traditional Chinese Medicine.

The Database supports training and advices in the daily work routine.

The computer program provides lists of recipes, ingredients and herbs, which are given to the client. individually adjustable according to patient's request from whole food to vegetarians (lacto, ovo, ...). For every register there is an information sheet which can be given to the client. All texts can be individually designed.

The syndromes can be combined and result in an intersection of the recommended recipes and ingredients. The automated diagnosis for the TCM enables you to check your experience during the training as well as to confirm your diagnosis in the working day. You select several predefined symptoms and have the program automatically display the relevant syndromes.

How to work with the database:
Select the patient / client, select one or more of the syndromes you diagnosed and print the folder.

You can change all values, create new symptoms or syndromes, develop recipes, change or adapt ingredients and herbs to your findings. In simple client management, all relevant data about the person is stored. You get an overview of the past diagnoses and the development of the course of the disease.

As a consultant you save a lot of time when you print out the recipe, food and herbal lists for the recognized syndromes and give them to the clients. You can use this time for a personal conversation. With the database, dieticians and nutritionists can view the nutrients and trace elements for each recipe and develop recipes for syndromes even with suggested ingredients.

All recipe and grocery lists can also be ordered from me as a combination of several diseases. I wish all readers good luck, health and happiness in life.
More information can be found at www.ebns.at.
Volunteer: www.krebsinfo.at
Josef Miligui